APPLIQUILT
IN THE CABIN

8 Fresh and Fun Designs

Tonee White

Martingale™
& COMPANY

CREDITS

President — Nancy J. Martin
CEO — Daniel J. Martin
Publisher — Jane Hamada
Editorial Director — Mary V. Green
Managing Editor — Tina Cook
Technical Editor — Karen Costello Soltys
Copy Editor — Allison A. Merrill
Design Director — Stan Green
Illustrator — Laurel Strand
Cover and Text Designer — Shelly Garrison
Photographer — Brent Kane

Martingale™
& COMPANY

That Patchwork Place®

That Patchwork Place® is an imprint of
Martingale & Company™.

Appliquilt in the Cabin: 8 Fresh and Fun Designs
© 2002 by Tonee White

Martingale & Company
20205 144th Avenue NE
Woodinville, WA 98072-8478 USA
www.martingale-pub.com

Printed in Hong Kong
07 06 05 04 03 02   8 7 6 5 4 3 2 1

MISSION STATEMENT
We are dedicated to providing quality products and service by working together to inspire creativity and to enrich the lives we touch.

Library of Congress Cataloging-in-Publication Data

White, Tonee
    Appliquilt in the cabin: 8 fresh and fun designs / Tonee White.
        p. cm.
    ISBN 1-56477-459-7
    1. Appliqué—Patterns. 2. Quilting—Patterns. 3. Log cabin quilts. I. Title.

    TT779 .W53 2002
    746.46'041—dc21

                                                    2002007829

DEDICATION

To Laurene Sinema, who has given me so much encouragement in my work

ACKNOWLEDGMENTS

I would like to thank my family—all of them—for their support. They have given me so much love, confidence, and freedom, which nurtures whatever creativity I possess.

CONTENTS

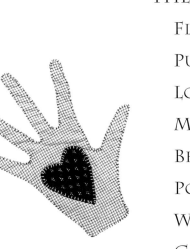

INTRODUCTION

SEVERAL YEARS ago, I wrote a few books for That Patchwork Place on my special technique, which I call "appliquilting." The idea was to use raw-edge appliqué shapes on top of a pieced background and to stitch them through all the quilt layers, not just the quilt top. The result was a folk-art look that lets you do the appliquéing (applying a design motif to a background) and quilting (sewing three or more layers together) in one step. Thus the name "appliquilting."

I am delighted to be following up those earlier books with a new take on my original technique. In this book, all the projects have two things in common. First, the designs begin with one form or another of the Log Cabin block, a particular favorite of mine. Second, the appliquilting is done not on raw edges as in the past but on edges that are turned under. In the quilts, I've used flannels and homespuns, which are more loosely woven than other quilting cottons, so turning the edges under using my needle-turn method is quite easy. I think you will find my new way of appliquilting to your liking.

After constructing a Log Cabin quilt, you will appliquilt motifs on the blocks using my needle-turn appliquilt stitch. (It resembles a blanket stitch but is much easier and faster.) Of course, you would be just as successful employing traditional construction and stitching techniques, but I hope you'll explore my method. I think it's quite fun.

For most of us, quilting is a recreational activity, so it should be enjoyable and stress-free. If you approach these projects and techniques with a positive attitude—knowing that they are easy and fun—you can't go wrong. Uneven stitches, less-than-sharp points, and less-than-smooth curves are all rarely noticed and perfectly acceptable. The eye sees the stitches, not the imperfections.

Enjoy the process and take a sense of pride in your accomplishment. Feel free to adapt the projects to suit your tastes. The finished quilt will be your masterpiece—I just provide the inspiration. Enjoy!

Tonee White

MATERIALS AND TOOLS

THE PROJECTS in this book do not require a lot of specialty tools or supplies. However, I do list the fabrics and supplies I used to achieve the distinctive look of the quilts. As always, use what works best for you, looking to the information below for guidance.

Fabrics

I used brushed homespun fabric for most of the quilts in this book. This type of fabric has a smooth, homespun side and a brushed reverse side that feels almost like flannel. Because the textures of the two sides are quite different, you can actually achieve contrast in a quilt by using the two different sides of just one fabric.

I also used flannel in the quilts. Flannel is a bit heavier than homespun, but these two fabrics work well together.

Not only are brushed homespuns and flannels soft and cozy choices for lap quilts, they're wonderful for appliqué too. Both fabrics are very soft and easy to manipulate, making it a snap to turn under the seam allowance in hand appliqué. If you've never used these fabrics for appliqué, I think you'll be pleasantly surprised.

You should know a few things about flannel and homespun before you try them. First, the weave is looser than on typical quilting cottons, so they tend to stretch. To make the fabrics easier to work with, I generally don't prewash them. Laundering washes away whatever sizing is in the fabric. When fabric is used right off the bolt, the sizing helps stabilize it during cutting and piecing.

Second, these fabrics shrink—especially flannel. If you plan to prewash your fabrics, you may need to allow a little extra yardage for shrinking. If you don't prewash, be aware that when you launder your quilt for the first time it will shrink and take on a slightly puckered, old-fashioned look. I find this look a perfect complement for warm, homespun fabrics, so I really don't mind.

One of the nice things about working with flannels and homespuns is that they are currently available in so many prints and patterns. From plaids and stripes to brights and pastels to primitive, contemporary, and even seasonal prints, just about any color or pattern you may want is available. Some manufacturers offer the same designs on their traditional cottons and on their brushed homespuns or flannels. I use them all, and many of my projects incorporate all three fabric types in the same quilt. The mix of textures just adds interest to the finished quilt.

Batting

I prefer lightweight cotton batting for several reasons. I find it's easier to needle—and when you're quilting through at least four layers as I do when I appliquilt, a thick batting is just too bulky to manipulate and stitch. Lightweight cotton batting also keeps the quilt from becoming too heavy. Remember, many of the quilts in this book are made from flannel, which is heavier than regular quilting cotton. And a lighter-weight batting makes a quilt more cuddly—one you'll enjoy snuggling under while reading a good book or watching an old black-and-white movie on television.

An alternative to cotton batting that seems to work quite nicely for wall hangings is Pellon fleece. This polyester product holds its shape and is very lightweight—so lightweight that you can see through it. Sometimes, however, I like to hang quilts on the wall to add to the decor, but

then I take them down to use on a cool evening. If I know I'm going to call one of my quilts into double duty, I still prefer cotton batting, simply because it's more conducive to snuggling.

Needles and Thread

From my first appliquilt project to the most recent, I have always wanted my hand stitching to be seen as part of the design. I began to look for thicker threads so the stitches would be more visible. Starting out, I used #8 pearl cotton and embroidery floss. Pearl cotton was not as readily available as floss, but I preferred the look that its tight twist provided. The strands of floss separated at times, which proved to be a nuisance.

A few years ago, a student of mine came to class with topstitching thread. Unlike floss and pearl cotton, topstitching thread comes on spools, which makes it easy to store. It doesn't separate like floss and is available in a fairly wide range of colors. I have used this thread extensively since. Two major thread manufacturers offer it, and I have found it at most chain fabric stores. Look for Mettler's topstitching thread or Gutterman's heavy-duty thread.

For a more rustic project, I use linen thread. Many quilt shops and craft stores sell this thread, which I think looks like a slender version of jute. It shows up nicely on the fuzzier fabrics. If you can't find linen thread at your local shop, try one of these sources:

The Quilted Apple
3043 North 24th Street
Phoenix, AZ 85016
(602) 956-0904

The Country Loft
4685 Date Street
La Mesa, CA 91941
(619) 466-5411

Another way of making your stitching more visible is to use a contrasting color when stitching motifs. I generally use several colors of thread in a quilt, choosing them to complement the fabrics. However, rather than matching the thread to a motif, I select a thread that will contrast with it. For example, I use green thread on a red apple and red thread on the apple's green leaf for more impact.

Choose a needle that will work with the type and weight of thread and fabric you'll be using. For the fabrics and threads I describe above, I prefer a size 6 or 7 embroidery/crewel needle. This is a sharp needle with an eye that can accommodate topstitching thread, three strands of floss, #8 pearl cotton, or the thinnest linen thread.

If you prefer a different type of needle, such as a Between or straw needle, by all means follow your preference. Whatever type of needle you choose, I recommend a size 6 or 7 to accommodate the thread.

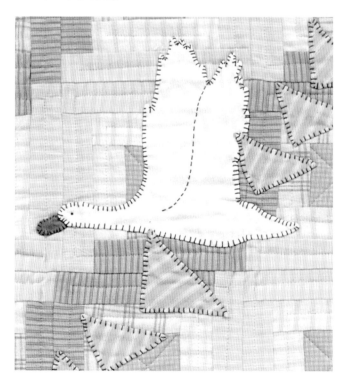

ALL OF the quilts in this book are made from variations on the traditional Log Cabin block. While each project has specific directions regarding fabric choices and cutting, the basic instructions given here apply to all of the projects.

The width of the strips and the dimensions of the block center vary from project to project. The number and width of strips to cut are given in each set of project directions. Strips are cut across the fabric, from selvage to selvage. The strips are then cut into shorter pieces, called "logs." The block center may or may not be the same width as the logs.

Traditionally, Log Cabin blocks have a light component and a dark component. Most, but not all, of these projects follow that format. Each project has a block diagram to show the piecing sequence, as well as a quilt layout diagram to show how to set the blocks (whether in a Barn Raising setting, a Straight Furrows setting, or some other arrangement).

The logs are sewn to the center square in a clockwise manner. After attaching one log to the center square, rotate the block a quarter turn (counterclockwise) before sewing on the next log.

Piecing a Log Cabin Block

Using a ¼" seam allowance and referring to the block diagram, follow the directions at right to piece a basic Log Cabin block.

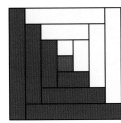

Basic Log Cabin Block

1. Sew a strip of the center fabric to a strip of the first log fabric along the long edges. Press the seam allowance toward the darker strip.

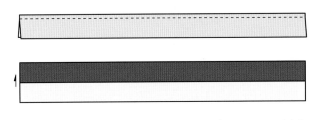

2. Cut the strip set into segments the same width as you cut the center strip, as shown.

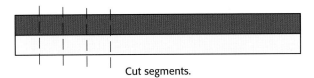

Cut segments.

3. Hold one of the segments cut in step 2 so that the log fabric is above the center square fabric. Lay a strip of the same log fabric, right sides together, on this segment, aligning right edges. Sew the strip to the segment along the right edge, stopping at the lower edge of the segment. Trim the strip even with the edge of the segment. Finger-press the seam open. Because of the thickness of flannel and brushed homespun, I press seams open to reduce bulk, but you may press seams to one side if you wish.

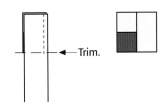

Trim.

4. Turn the developing block a quarter turn to the left. Choose a new fabric for the remaining 2 sides of the round. Lay a strip of the new fabric, right sides together, on top of the

pieced unit so it is aligned with the short end of the last log added and the center square, as shown. Sew the strip to the pieced unit, trim, and finger press as in step 3.

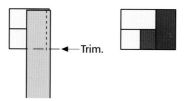

← Trim.

5. Rotate the unit a quarter turn to the left. Using the same fabric as in the previous log, place a strip along the right edge of the block. Sew, trim, and press.

6. One round is now completed. (Logs are sewn to all 4 sides of the center square.) Press the seams with an iron before adding the next round of logs.

Round 1

7. Round 2 is a repeat of round 1, except that instead of a single square of fabric as the block center, you now have a pieced square. You may or may not change fabrics with each round. The Log Cabin blocks in some projects are scrappy; others use just 2 log fabrics.

Scrappy Log Cabin Block

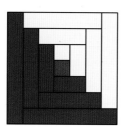

Plain Log Cabin Block

TIP

KEEPING THE SEQUENCE

You can add as many rounds as you want to Log Cabin blocks, but project directions will specify how many are used in specific projects. No matter how many rounds you are adding, when you are ready to add the next log, position the last log added at the top of the unit. Sew the first log of the new round to the right side of the first log of the previous round.

ASSEMBLING AND QUILTING

WHILE ALL the projects in the book include appliqué, my technique is to add the appliqué last so that the appliqué stitches also work as the quilting stitches. This means that before you complete the appliqué you need to assemble the blocks, add the borders, and layer and baste the quilt. I typically do basic machine quilting at this stage, too.

Quilt Assembly

All the projects in this book are assembled in the same way: the blocks are set in horizontal rows, which are sewn together to make the quilt top. It's the orientation of the blocks that makes the designs look different. Vertical zigzags or chevrons can be achieved simply by rotating the blocks differently. Each project has a quilt layout diagram to help you orient the blocks correctly. Pay careful attention to these, because some of the projects have blocks with different color configurations and rotations.

Following the quilt layout diagram, sew the blocks together and add the borders as instructed. When the quilt top is complete, give it one final pressing.

Layering and Basting

Firmly attach the backing right side down to a flat surface such as a table or floor. You can use large office clamps to attach the backing to a table; masking tape works well on either floors or tables. If you don't have a large table, check with your local quilt shop. Many shops allow quilters to use their classroom tables for basting when classes aren't in session.

Lay the batting on top of the backing and smooth it from the center to the outer edges to remove any wrinkles or creases. Center your quilt top on the batting, and again smooth from the center out.

If you are planning to machine quilt, I suggest pin-basting the three layers together. Using medium-size safety pins, pin a grid of 4" to 6", starting in the middle and working your way out to the edges and smoothing as you go. I don't close the safety pins until they have all been placed, since you can disturb the backing slightly when you close a pin. When you multiply that small disturbance by the number of pins used, it ends up being not so small. If closing so many pins is hard on your fingers, check your quilt shop for a tool made just for that purpose.

If you plan to hand quilt, I suggest you baste with thread. Thread basting holds the layers together a little more securely. If you lap quilt, your piece is not necessarily as flat as it would be on a sewing-machine table. You need the extra hold that thread basting gives to keep the layers from shifting. Besides, if you use a hoop or frame, the safety pins will interfere.

Basting needles can be found at most quilt shops. They have larger eyes and are longer than most needles. You can work with a longer thread, too, to save the time of frequently rethreading your needle. I usually use a bright or contrasting color thread, which is easier to remove when the quilting is complete because it's easy to spot.

Baste in a 3" to 4" grid, beginning in the middle of the quilt top. To save time, use large stitches. I usually don't even bother to knot the end of the thread! Thread basting can be removed as you complete an area or all at once when all the quilting is finished.

Quilting

Before I start machine quilting my three-layer "sandwich," I increase the stitch length from 2.5 to 3.5 on my sewing machine to help prevent gathering and puckering. I fill four or five bobbins with thread to match the backing so I don't have to break the quilting rhythm I get into merely to wind a new bobbin.

I also make sure the entire quilt will be supported while I am quilting. If part of it hangs off the table, drag is created, which can prevent a finished quilt from hanging straight. If your machine is on a small table, you might be better off moving it to a larger table, such as a dining room table, or placing other tables around the smaller one. Your ironing board can work well as a quilt support if you lower it to the height of your sewing table.

I make sure my walking foot is operational. A walking foot comes either as an attachment or built into your machine. Unless you're doing free-motion quilting, I strongly advise against quilting without one. A walking foot feeds the top of the sandwich through the stitching process just as the feed dogs move the backing fabric. With the bulk of the sandwich, you need a walking foot to help feed it through evenly.

Adequate basting, in combination with feed dogs and a walking foot, helps insure a pucker-free quilt.

I quilt through the lengthwise center of all logs, using invisible thread on top of my machine so I don't have to worry about color changes. In the bobbin, I use 50-weight cotton thread that matches the backing fabric. If you wish to conceal the thread on the quilt back, use a busy print for the quilt backing, and the quilting stitches won't be very visible.

Begin stitching in the center of the top edge of the sandwich and stitch all the vertical lines, tacking at the beginning and end of each sewn line to secure the threads. After all the lines have been stitched in one direction, turn the piece so you can quilt the logs going in the perpendicular direction. Stitch them the same way, starting and stopping at the existing stitching, tacking as before.

It is especially important to secure the starting and stopping points when using invisible thread because this type of thread tends to pull out. If your machine does not have a tack stitch, sew three to four stitches, backstitch three to four stitches, and continue. When reaching the end of a line of quilting, backstitch three to four stitches to secure the thread.

NEEDLE-TURN appliqué is exactly what it sounds like. You use the tip of your needle to turn under the raw edge of the appliqué shape and stitch it in place. To determine where to turn under the fabric, you need a clear outline of the motif marked on the right side of the fabric. You can mark the appliqué outline using templates cut from either plastic or freezer paper. I prefer plastic templates. They're more durable, which means I can save them in my files. On occasion, I reuse the designs.

However, there are many ways to prepare your motifs for appliqué. If you have a favorite method other than needle-turn, by all means use it. Your comfort level is important. The only method that won't work with appliquilting is using freezer paper on the *wrong* side of the appliqué shape, because to remove the template you would have to cut through not only the background fabric but the quilt backing and batting, too.

Using Plastic Templates

1. For each appliqué motif, trace the pattern onto template plastic. Cut out the template on the drawn lines.

2. Place the template on the right side of the appropriate fabric, at least ¼" to ⅓" from the edges. Trace around the template with a pencil or permanent pen. I prefer a lead pencil for light fabrics and a white or pastel pencil for dark fabrics.

3. Cut out the motif, leaving a ¼" seam allowance all around the outside of the marked line, as shown.

Cut out shape,
leaving ¼" seam allowance.

Using Freezer-Paper Templates

1. For each individual appliqué needed, trace the pattern onto the dull side of freezer paper. Cut out the template on the drawn line.

2. Using a dry iron, press the template to the right side of the appliqué fabric, with the shiny side of the paper face down on the fabric.

3. There are 2 ways to proceed. First, you can trace around the paper as described in step 2 of "Using Plastic Templates" at left, then remove the paper and cut out the shape ¼" from the traced line. Or, like some of my students, you can use the edge of the freezer paper as your guide when you cut out the shape ¼" from the edge and when you turn the seam allowance under, eliminating the need to draw a guideline.

Freezer paper

Cut out shape,
leaving ¼" seam allowance.

Needle-Turn Appliquilt Stitch

IN TRADITIONAL appliqué, you stitch a fabric motif to another piece of fabric. In appliquilt, you stitch a fabric motif to a three-layered quilt sandwich made up of backing fabric, batting, and quilt top.

For appliquilting, I recommend heavy-duty thread and strong, sharp needles. I do not use a quilt frame, although that is perfectly acceptable if it is comfortable for you. If you use a thimble for regular hand quilting, you will probably want to use one for this stitching too.

Knot the end of your thread and bring your needle up from the back of the appliqué motif ⅛" to ¼" inside the traced line. Using the tip of your needle, tuck under the seam allowance of the appliqué shape along the traced line or along the edge of the freezer paper. Turn under only about 1" to 2" ahead of your starting point. Stitch down into the quilt sandwich right next to the folded edge, as shown.

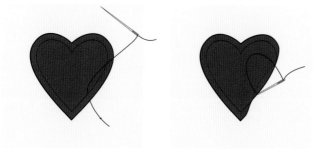

When you feel the tip of the needle touch your finger underneath the quilt backing, pop the needle up, taking a small bite of the backing fabric and then traveling through the batting at a 45° angle. Bring the needle up through the appliqué ⅛" to ¼" ahead of the previous stitch and about ⅛" to ¼" inside the edge of the appliqué shape. Note that this stitch, which is really a type of overcast stitch, is larger than the typical, almost invisible appliqué stitch. In this method you want the thread to show as a design element. Note that this stitch also differs from

traditional quilting, where the needle travels through the sandwich at 90° (perpendicular to the sandwich), so that the stitches are the same size on the top and the bottom. In appliquilting the needle travels through the sandwich at 45°, resulting in stitches that are larger on the top and smaller on the bottom. You certainly may use the traditional quilting stitch to attach the appliqués if that is your habit; I happen to prefer smaller stitches on the back of my work.

Appliquilt Stitch

The place where you bring your needle up through the appliqué determines the "look" of your project. I generally bring my needle up ⅛" to ¼" inside the folded edge or traced line, so that my stitches show on top of the appliqués. Using thread in a contrasting color allows the stitches to be seen clearly, as discussed under "Needles and Thread" on page 6. This stitch looks very much like a blanket stitch, but I find my overcast stitch, or mock blanket stitch, is easier and faster to do. And it gives a more primitive or country look to the finished piece.

For a more polished or traditional look, bring the needle up through the appliqué right on the traced line and then right back down through the sandwich just next to the "up" stitch. This will conceal your stitches, rather than making them visible as part of the design. To make your stitches even less noticeable, match the thread to the fabric of the appliqué piece as closely as possible.

A NUMBER of the projects in this book include vines and stems, most of which finish at ½" wide. A bias tape maker is a handy tool to have to make these vines and stems, and I highly recommend it. From a 1"-wide strip of fabric, you can quickly and easily make a ½"-wide stem with folded edges.

You don't always need bias strips to make twining vines, however. You'll find that brushed homespun fabric is flexible enough to make gentle curves, such as those of the vines in "Morning Glories" on page 41. To make these vines, cut 1"-wide strips across the width of the fabric, from selvage to selvage.

For sharper curves I use bias strips, but they don't have to be cut on a true 45° angle. Fold a quarter-yard piece of fabric in half diagonally from the upper left corner to the lower right corner. Press this crease and then cut along the crease. You will have cut across the grain line but at less than a 45° angle. Cut your strips following the diagonal cut you just made and your vines will curve nicely and lie flat against your quilt.

For the narrow stems in "Morning Glories," I cut strips 6" to 8" long and ¾" wide. After pinning a strip in place on the quilt, right sides together, I stitched the stem along one edge using a small running stitch and a scant ¼" seam allowance. Then I folded the unsewn edge of the strip over the stitched side, exposing the right side of the fabric. I turned under the raw edge of the strip and appliquéd it in place. I prefer this method for narrow stems, as I have not had much success with the ¼" bias tape maker. This method lets you achieve thin stems quite easily.

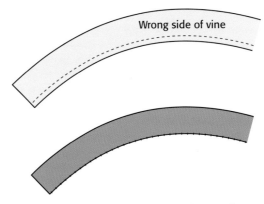

Flip over and fold under raw edge; stitch.

I USED traditional binding for all the quilts in this book. There are many different ways to bind a quilt. As with appliqué methods, there is no right or wrong way, only different. If you have a favorite method, please use it. I cut binding strips 2½" wide from selvage to selvage. The number of strips needed for each project is given in the quilt cutting directions.

1. Machine sew the binding strips together, end to end. Press the seam allowances open to reduce bulk. Fold the long strip in half lengthwise, with wrong sides together and raw edges aligned. Press the fold well.

2. I do not trim excess batting and backing until the binding has been stitched to all edges. Beginning near the center of the bottom edge of the quilt, pin the raw edges of the binding along the raw edge of the quilt top, leaving free a tail approximately 8" long.

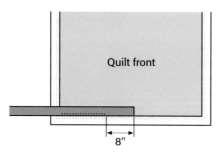

3. Using a ¼" seam allowance, stitch to within ¼" of the first corner. Backtack and cut the threads. Take the quilt from the machine and turn it a quarter turn. Fold the unsewn binding into a miter at the corner, as shown. Fold the binding back down along the side edge of the quilt. Beginning again at the corner, stitch the binding to the quilt as described above, again stopping ¼" before the next corner.

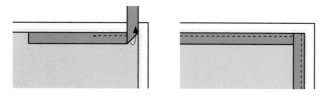

4. Continue stitching and mitering corners. Stop stitching and backtack approximately 12" from where you began on the bottom of the quilt. You should have a tail of binding left.

5. With your fingers, walk the 2 binding tails along the edge of the quilt until they meet. Holding both tails with the unstitched binding flat against the quilt edge, pin the tails together where they meet. Stitch the tails together at this point, from the folded edge to the raw edge. Trim the tails to about ½". Finger-press the tails to each side of the seam.

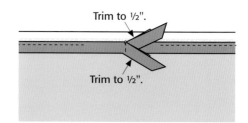

6. Pin the unstitched binding to the edge of the quilt top. Stitch.

7. Trim the excess batting and backing so they are even with edges of the quilt top and binding. Turn the folded edge of the binding to the back of the quilt. Adjust the mitered corners, and whipstitch the folded edge of the binding to the back of the quilt.

SOFT BLUE and yellow Log Cabin blocks set in a chevron pattern mimic the formations of geese flying south for the winter. Appliquilted "real" geese and darker blue and yellow triangles tie the whole design together. To make the large-scale plaid border stand out, a narrow piping of a darker plaid is used to separate the border from the blocks. This is a neat design trick that mimics the look of the binding.

Finished quilt size: 44" x 56"
Finished block size: 6" x 6"

Materials

Yardages are based on 40"-wide fabric.

1 yd. large-scale plaid for border
⅔ yd. yellow ticking for logs
½ yd. blue ticking for logs
½ yd. white flannel for geese appliqués
½ yd. yellow-and-white plaid for logs
⅓ yd. blue-and-white plaid for logs
¼ yd. yellow-and-blue check for block centers
¼ yd. *each* of dark yellow plaid and dark blue plaid for triangle appliqués
Scrap of orange flannel for geese appliqués
2¾ yds. fabric for backing
⅔ yd. medium blue plaid for piping and binding
48" x 60" piece of batting

Cutting

All fabric strips are cut across the grain of the fabric. All cut sizes allow for ¼" seam allowances.

Fabric	Used For	Number to Cut	Size to Cut
Yellow-and-blue check	Block centers	3 strips	2½" wide
Blue-and-white plaid	First round of logs	8 strips	1½" wide
Yellow-and-white plaid	First round of logs	10 strips	1½" wide
Blue ticking	Second round of logs	12 strips	1½" wide
Yellow ticking	Second round of logs	15 strips	1½" wide
Medium blue plaid	Piping	6 strips	1" wide
	Binding	5 strips	2½" wide
Large-scale plaid	Border	5 strips	4½" wide

Making the Blocks

All the blocks in this quilt are identical. Following instructions in "Log Cabin Block Construction" on page 7, make 48 blocks, starting with a yellow-and-blue check center surrounded by 2 rounds of logs. The first round is made up of 2 blue-and-white plaid logs, followed by 2 yellow-and-white plaid logs. For the second round, add 2 blue ticking logs, followed by 2 yellow ticking logs. Your blocks should measure 6½" with seam allowances.

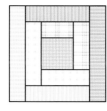

Log Cabin Block
Make 48.

Assembling the Quilt

1. Following the quilt layout diagram below, sew the blocks into 8 rows of 6 blocks each.

Quilt Layout

2. To prepare the piping, sew the five 1" medium blue plaid strips together, end to end. Press the seams open. Fold the long strip in half lengthwise, wrong sides together, and press.

3. Measure the width of the quilt top and trim 2 of the large-scale plaid border strips to this length. From the piping, cut 2 pieces to the same length. Lay 1 of the cut piping strips along the top edge of quilt. Then place 1 of the trimmed border strips on top of the piping strip, right sides together, so that the raw edges of the quilt top, piping, and border are all aligned. Pin layers together and stitch.

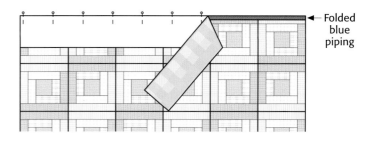

Folded blue piping

4. Open the seam and press. Press the piping toward the blocks and the border away from the blocks.

5. Repeat, sewing the remaining cut piping strip and trimmed border strip to the bottom edge of the quilt top.

6. For the side borders, measure the length of the quilt top. Sew the remaining 3 border strips together end to end. From the long strip, cut 2 side border strips the same length as your quilt top. From the remaining piping strip, cut 2 pieces to the length of just the blocks plus 2" (the piping does not extend along the edges of the top and bottom borders).

   Open the folded piping strips, fold under 1" at each short end, then refold the strips and press. Pin the piping strips to the sides of the quilt. Then place the border strips on top of the piping strips and quilt top with all raw edges aligned. Stitch. Press as in step 4.

Finishing the Quilt

Follow the directions for quilting in "Assembling and Quilting" on page 9.

1. Piece the backing, and then layer the backing, batting, and quilt top; pin baste.

2. Quilt. I machine quilted through the lengthwise center of each log and quilted an X through the center square of each block.

3. You may bind your quilt now or after the appliquilting is finished; see "Binding" on page 14.

> **TIP**
>
> ### PIECED BACKINGS
>
> While you can simply purchase the yardage required for your quilt and sew two lengths of it together to make a backing large enough, sometimes it is fun to use leftovers from the quilt top. For this quilt, I used some of my extra blue and yellow plaid fabrics to make strips of large-scale flying-geese units. I sewed these strips to other long strips of flannel to make an interesting and theme-appropriate backing. If you don't want to do a lot of extra piecing, you can simply sew together fat quarters or large squares or rectangles to make use of your leftovers. They'll coordinate perfectly with the quilt top and put to use fabrics that might otherwise languish in your scrap basket.

Appliquilting

1. Referring to "Preparing the Appliqué Motifs" on page 11 and using the patterns on pages 19–23, cut and prepare 1 each of the 5 geese from the white flannel. Cut their bills from the orange flannel. From the dark blue plaid,

cut 16 A triangles and 14 B triangles; from the dark yellow plaid, cut 12 A triangles and 12 B triangles.

2. Place the geese and triangle appliqués on the quilt, referring to the photograph on page 15 and the quilt plan below.

Quilt Plan

3. Following the instructions in "Needle-Turn Appliquilt Stitch" on page 12, sew the motifs to your quilt by using navy thread for the geese and yellow triangles and yellow thread for the blue triangles.

4. Using a running stitch through all quilt layers, stitch the wing detail on the goose wings with navy thread, following the dashed lines on the patterns. To hide the knots, begin by slipping the threaded needle between the appliquilt stitches on the edge of the motif and coming up at one end of the line. Tie off the stitching on the quilt back.

5. Be sure to label your quilt, and add a hanging sleeve if desired.

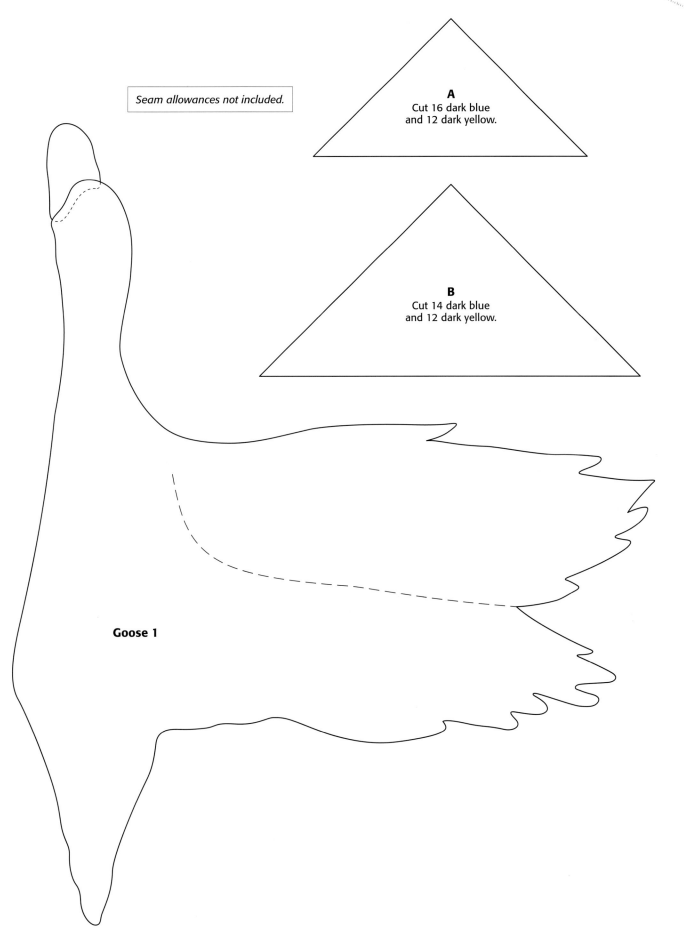

Seam allowances not included.

A
Cut 16 dark blue
and 12 dark yellow.

B
Cut 14 dark blue
and 12 dark yellow.

Goose 1

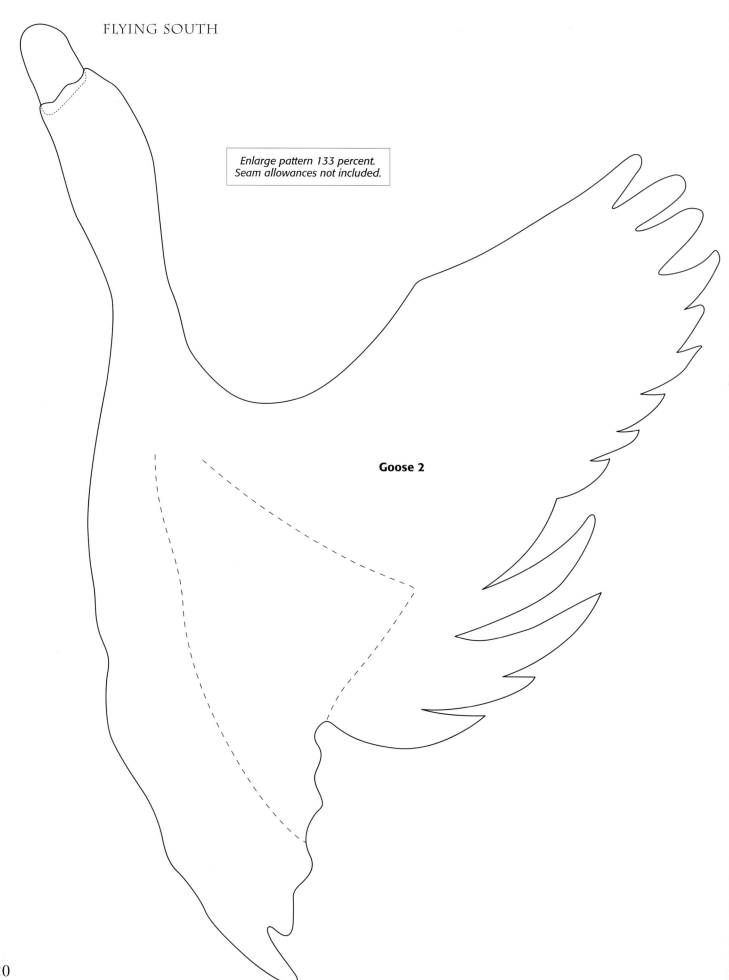

Enlarge pattern 133 percent.
Seam allowances not included.

Goose 2

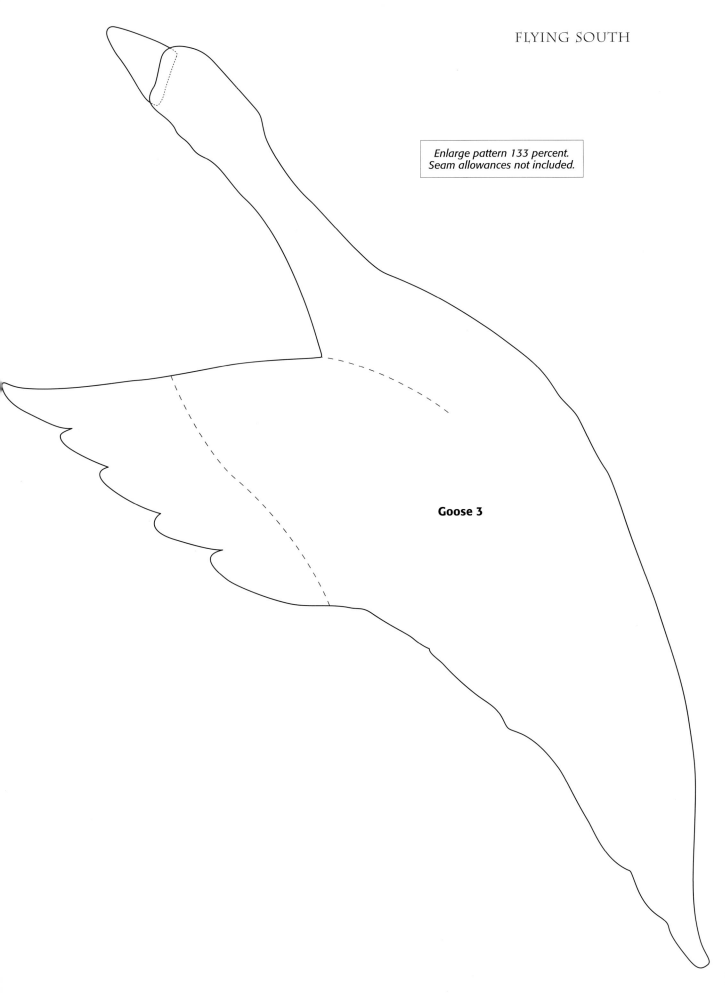

Enlarge pattern 133 percent.
Seam allowances not included.

Goose 3

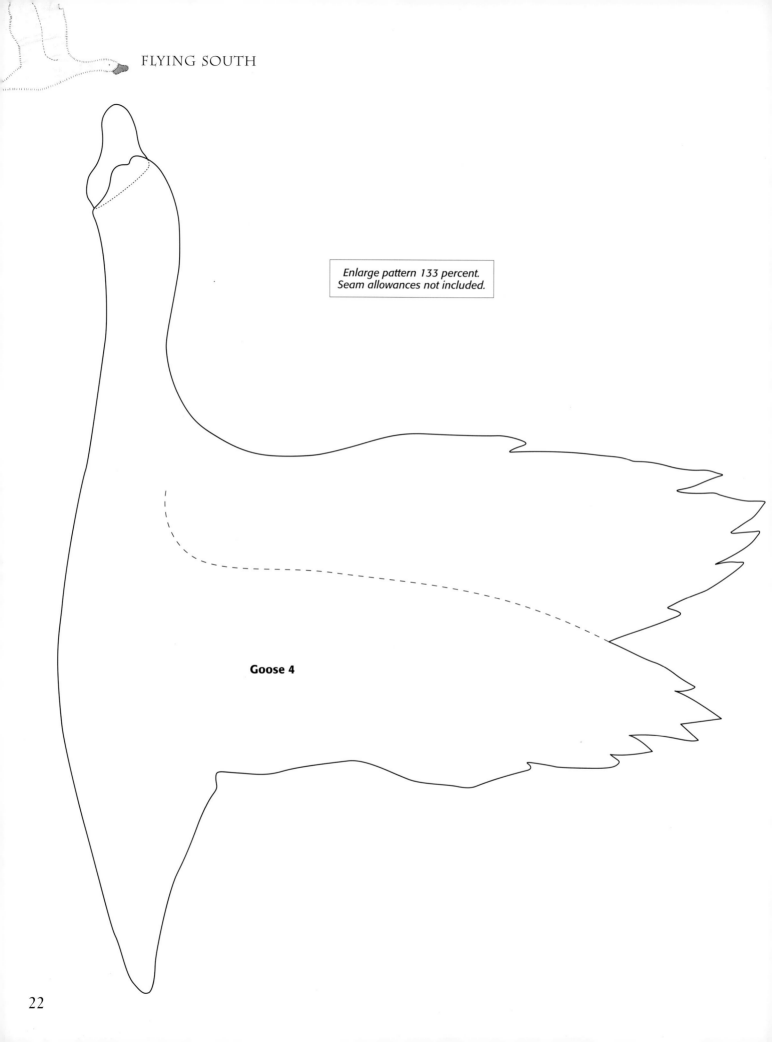

Enlarge pattern 133 percent.
Seam allowances not included.

Goose 4

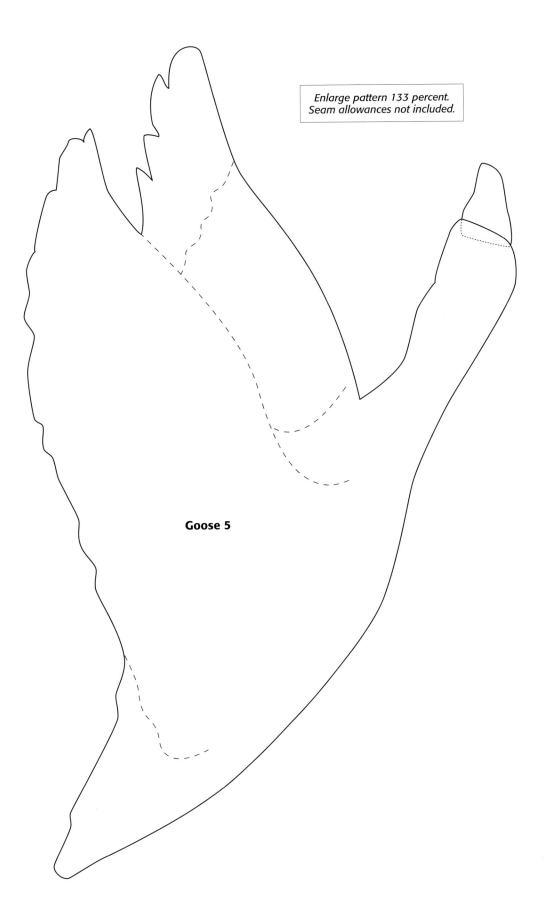

Enlarge pattern 133 percent.
Seam allowances not included.

Goose 5

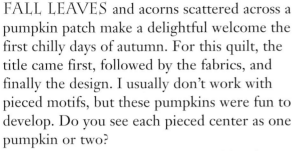

FALL LEAVES and acorns scattered across a pumpkin patch make a delightful welcome the first chilly days of autumn. For this quilt, the title came first, followed by the fabrics, and finally the design. I usually don't work with pieced motifs, but these pumpkins were fun to develop. Do you see each pieced center as one pumpkin or two?

Each 8" pumpkin is surrounded by three rounds of logs. To emphasize the pattern, I used narrow plaid sashing strips that I call "zingers." Cut from bold fabrics, the zingers lead your eye in a stair-step fashion across the quilt.

Finished quilt size: 54½" x 69½"
Finished block size: 14" x 14"

Materials

Yardages are based on 40"-wide fabric.

1½ yds. black solid for logs, border, and binding
½ yd. *each* of 2 light prints for logs
⅝ yd. beige solid for pumpkin backgrounds
⅝ yd. allover print for border
¾ yd. *total* of at least 8 assorted oranges for pumpkins
½ yd. bright orange plaid for sashing
½ yd. *total* of 2 dark prints for logs
¼ yd. bright green plaid for sashing
¼ yd. black plaid for sashing
¼ yd. green for vines and leaves
⅛ yd. *each* of several golds, yellows, and oranges for leaf, triangle, acorn, and berry appliqués
Scrap or ⅛ yd. of dark brown for stem appliqués
3⅜ yds. fabric for backing
59" x 74" piece of batting
48" of narrow black braid or embroidery floss

Cutting

All fabric strips are cut across the grain of the fabric, except where noted. All cut sizes allow for ¼" seam allowances.

Fabric	Used For	Number to Cut	Size to Cut
Beige solid	Pumpkin corners	88 squares	1½" x 1½"
	Pumpkin backgrounds	8 rectangles	1½" x 4½"
	First round of logs	6 strips	1½" wide
Assorted oranges	Pumpkins	17 rectangles	4½" x 8½"
	Pumpkins	7 rectangles	4½" x 7½"
Black solid	First round of logs	6 strips	1½" wide
	Left border	1 lengthwise strip	4½" x 26½"
	Top border	1 lengthwise strip	4½" x 55½"
	Right border	1 lengthwise strip	4½" x 45½"
	Flying geese in border	6 squares	2½" x 2½"
		5 rectangles	2½" x 4½"
	Binding	7 strips	2½" wide
Light print #1	Second round of logs	7 strips	1½" wide
Dark print #1	Second round of logs	8 strips	1½" wide
Light print #2	Third round of logs	8 strips	1½" wide
Dark print #2	Third round of logs	9 strips	1½" wide
Bright orange plaid	Sashing	16 strips	1½" x 14½"
Bright green plaid	Sashing	8 strips	1½" x 14½"
Black plaid	Sashing	7 strips	1½" x 14½"
Allover print	Left border	1 strip	4½" x 29½"
	Bottom border	1 lengthwise strip	4½" x 55½"
	Right border	1 rectangle	4½" x 6½"
	Flying geese in border	10 squares	2½" x 2½"
	Flying geese in border	3 rectangles	2½" x 4½"

Making the Blocks

Some of the pumpkins are pieced with 2 different fabrics, and some have one half that's taller than the other. I made 5 pumpkins even across the top and 7 uneven. You can choose any combination for your quilt; simply adjust the cutting instructions accordingly.

1. Draw a diagonal line on all 1½" beige solid squares with a pencil or fine-tip permanent marker.

2. Place a solid square on each corner of the 4½" x 8½" orange rectangles as shown. For the 4½" x 7½" orange rectangles, place a solid square on 3 of the corners as shown. Four of the shorter rectangles don't get a square on the upper right corner; the other 3 don't get a square on the upper left corner. Make sure the marked lines are oriented as shown.

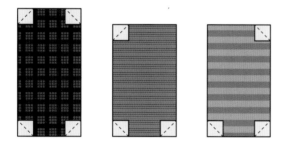

3. For each orange rectangle in step 2, stitch on the drawn line on the solid squares. Fold back the resulting triangle to align with edges of the orange block and press. Cut away the solid triangle that lies between the top triangle and the orange rectangle (leaving a ¼" seam allowance) to reduce bulk.

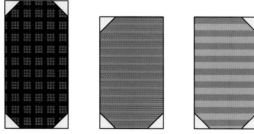

Make 17.   Make 4.   Make 3.

4. Sew the 4½" x 8½" orange rectangles together in pairs along their 8½" edges. Be sure to include the corner triangles in these seams. Press the seam allowances to one side. Make 5 of these pumpkin units.

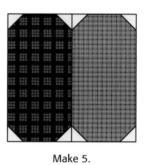

Make 5.

5. Sew a 1½" x 4½" beige solid rectangle to the top of each 4½" x 7½" orange rectangle, right sides together. Press the seam allowances toward the orange fabric. Make 7 of these units.

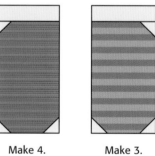

Make 4.   Make 3.

6. Sew the 7 remaining 4½" x 8½" orange rectangles to the units constructed in step 5, as shown. Make sure the top corner without a solid triangle is facing toward the center of the block and not the outside edge. Press the seam allowances toward the 8½" orange rectangles.

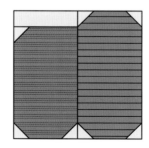

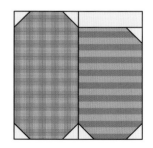

Make 4.   Make 3.

7. The centers of the Log Cabin blocks in this quilt are the 8½" pumpkins. Lay a beige solid strip along the right side of a pumpkin, right sides together, and stitch the strip to the block. Trim the strip even with the bottom edge of the pumpkin. This is the first log of the first round. Continue sewing the logs by following instructions in "Log Cabin Block Construction" on page 7, beginning with step 3.

Assembling the Quilt

1. Referring to the quilt layout below, lay out the Log Cabin pumpkin blocks and plaid sashing strips, paying careful attention to color placement of the sashing strips.

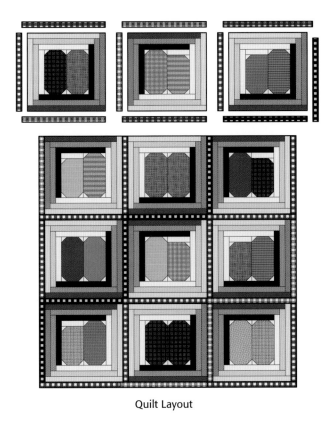

Quilt Layout

2. Sew the blocks and sashing strips together in horizontal rows. Then sew the rows together. Press.

Making the Pieced Border

1. Draw a diagonal line on the wrong side of each 2½" allover print square with a pencil or fine-tip permanent marker.

2. Place a 2½" allover print square at 1 end of a 2½" x 4½" black rectangle, right sides together. Stitch on the drawn line. Fold back the resulting triangle to align with the edges of the black rectangle and press. Cut away the triangle that lies between the allover print triangle and the black rectangle (leaving a ¼" seam allowance) to reduce bulk. Make 5 of these units.

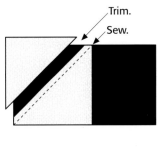

3. Place another 2½" allover print square on the other end of the black rectangle, as shown. Stitch on the diagonal line, trim, and press as in step 2. Repeat to make 5 flying-geese units.

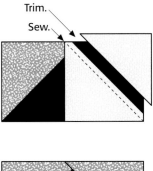

Make 5.

4. Sew the 5 flying-geese units together along the 4½" edges and with the black triangles pointing in the same direction. Attach this unit to the end of the 4½" x 45½" black border strip, with the triangles pointing away from the border strip. Press the seam allowances toward the border strip.

5. To complete the right border, sew the 4½" x 6½" allover print rectangle to the opposite end of the flying-geese unit. Press the seam allowance away from the flying-geese unit. Sew the border to the right side of the quilt top. Press the seam allowance toward the border.

Right Border

6. Make 3 more flying-geese units by using the 2½" black solid squares and the 2½" x 4½" allover print rectangles, referring to steps 1–3 on page 27. These flying-geese units are made in the same manner, but the positions of the 2 fabrics are reversed. Sew the flying-geese units together so the triangles point in the same direction.

7. Sew this flying-geese unit between the 4½" x 26½" black solid strip and the 4½" x 29½" allover print strip to complete the left border. The flying-geese units should be pointing toward the black strip. Press the seam allowances away from the flying-geese units. Sew this border to the left side of the quilt top. Press the seam allowance toward the border.

Left Border

8. Sew the 4½" x 55½" black solid border strip to the top of the quilt top and the 4½" x 55½" allover print border strip to the bottom of the quilt top. Press seam allowances toward the borders.

Finishing the Quilt

Follow the directions for quilting in "Assembling and Quilting" on page 9.

1. Piece the quilt backing, and then layer the backing, batting, and quilt top; pin baste.

2. Quilt. I machine quilted the pumpkins using invisible thread (monofilament) in a large meandering pattern. I quilted the logs lengthwise through their centers.

3. You may bind your quilt now or after the appliquilting is finished; see "Binding" on page 14. Be sure to label your quilt.

Appliquilting

1. Referring to "Preparing the Appliqué Motifs" on page 11 and using the appliqué patterns on pages 30–33, cut and prepare 12 pumpkin stems, approximately 40 various leaves, 8 acorns, 19 triangles, and 16 berries. Refer to the quilt photograph on page 24 for color ideas, or mix and match colors as desired.

2. Following the directions for "Vines and Stems" on page 13, make approximately 70" of ½"-wide vines.

3. Place the appliqués on the quilt, referring to the quilt plan on page 29 and the quilt photograph. Use your creativity to arrange as many appliqué motifs as you'd like. My quilt is merely a suggestion.

4. Following the instructions in "Needle-Turn Appliquilt Stitch" on page 12, sew the motifs to the quilt using a light-colored thread.

5. For the pumpkin tendrils, use a couching technique to stitch 4" to 6" lengths of either a narrow black braid or 6 strands of embroidery floss to the quilt. Refer to the tip box at right for information on couching.

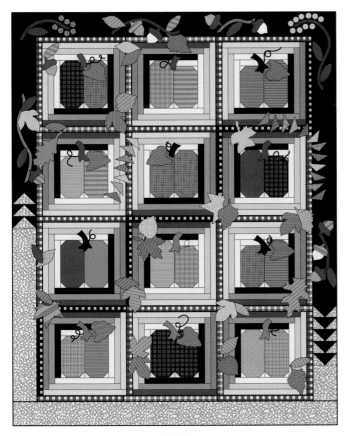

Quilt Plan

TIP

COUCHING BY HAND OR MACHINE

Narrow braid or embroidery floss can easily be attached to a quilt by hand or machine using a couching stitch. For either method, pin the braid in place with straight pins, making sure to pin curves smoothly.

For hand couching, use black sewing thread knotted at one end. Bring the needle up from the back of the quilt so that it is next to one end of the braid or floss. Send your needle back down through all the layers just on the opposite side of the braid or floss. Continue with stitches approximately ⅛" apart.

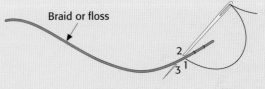

Braid or floss

Couching by Hand

For machine couching, use monofilament in the needle and regular sewing thread in the bobbin. Set the machine to a very narrow zigzag stitch, and sew from one end of the tendril to the other, making sure the zigzag swings from one side of the braid or floss to the other. Secure the starting and ending stitch by taking very tiny stitches or backstitching.

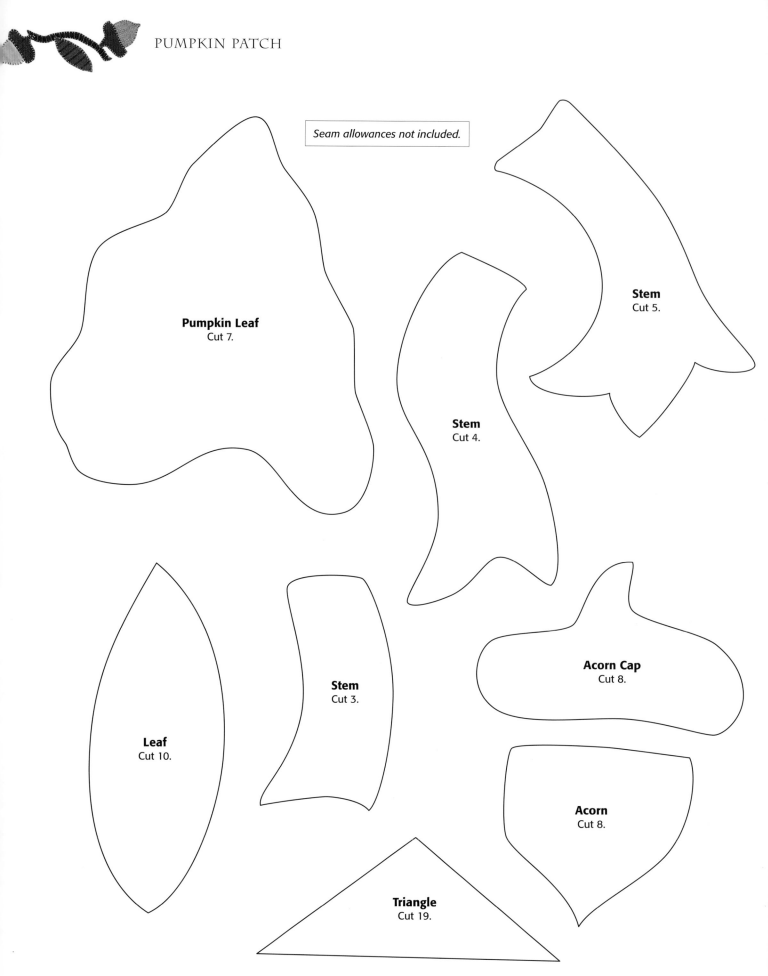

Seam allowances not included.

Pumpkin Leaf
Cut 7.

Stem
Cut 5.

Stem
Cut 4.

Stem
Cut 3.

Acorn Cap
Cut 8.

Leaf
Cut 10.

Acorn
Cut 8.

Triangle
Cut 19.

Seam allowances not included.

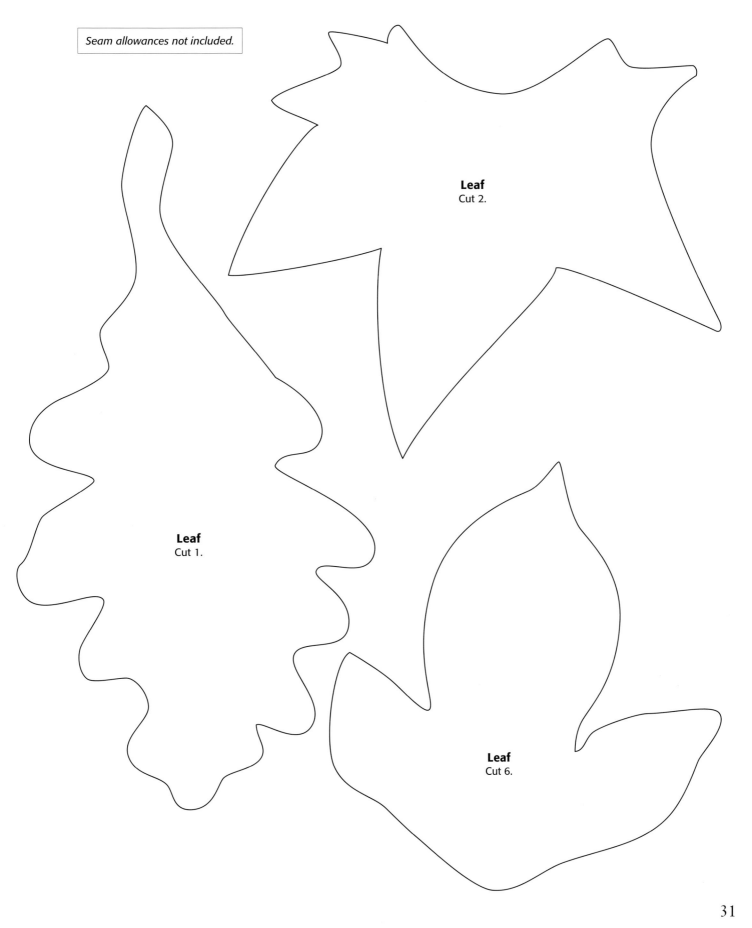

Leaf
Cut 2.

Leaf
Cut 1.

Leaf
Cut 6.

Seam allowances not included.

Leaf
Cut 3.

Leaf
Cut 1.

Leaf
Cut 1.

Leaf
Cut 5.

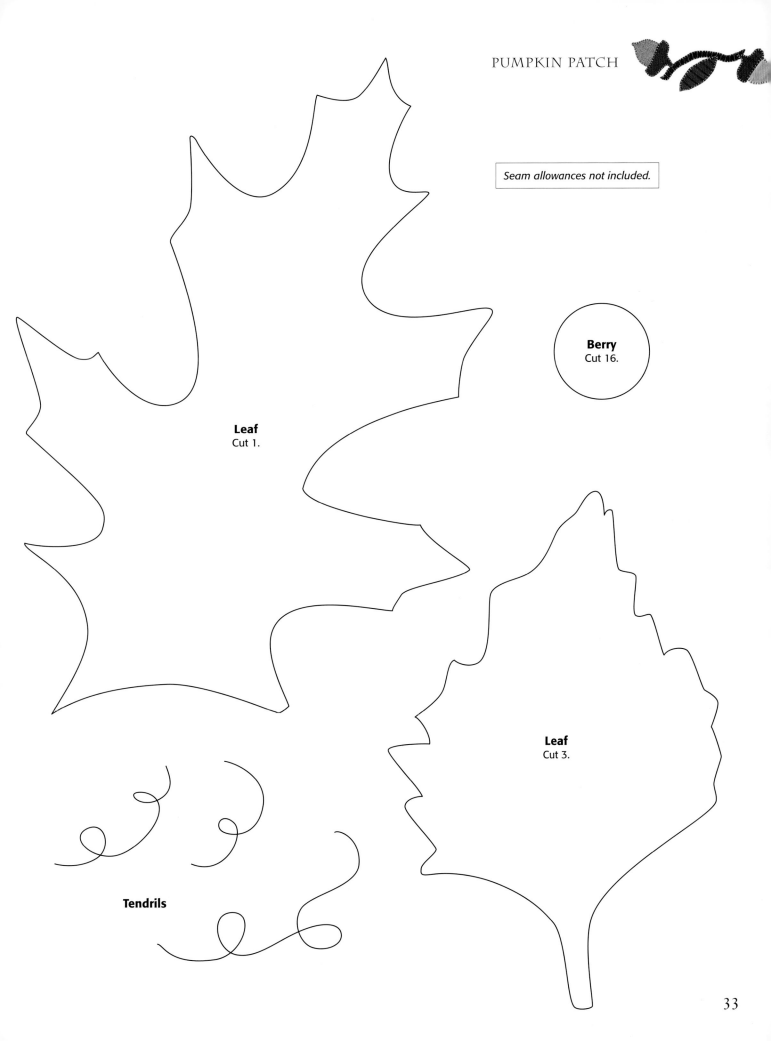

Seam allowances not included.

Berry
Cut 16.

Leaf
Cut 1.

Leaf
Cut 3.

Tendrils

THIS BRIGHT and cheery quilt offers a taste of Americana. Use it for a Fourth of July picnic or to chase the chill while watching fireworks. This quilt also makes a welcome gift for a child. I made my first quilt in this pattern for a toddler, knowing it would be appropriate for his whole childhood and beyond.

Finished quilt size: 42½" x 60½"
Finished block size: 6" x 6"

Materials

Yardages are based on 40"-wide fabric.

¾ yd. light blue for blocks
¾ yd. red for blocks
¾ yd. dark blue for blocks
¾ yd. light check for blocks
⅝ yd. light red for blocks
⅝ yd. red gingham for blocks and binding
⅜ yd. red plaid for blocks
¼ yd. gold solid for star and flag appliqués
¼ yd. dark blue plaid for blocks
2¾ yds. fabric for backing
47" x 65" piece of batting

Cutting

All fabric strips are cut across the grain of the fabric. All cut sizes allow for ¼" seam allowances.

Fabric	Used For	Number to Cut	Size to Cut
Dark blue plaid	Small Flag blocks	1 strip	3½" wide
	Large Flag block	1 rectangle	4½" x 6½"
Red	Small and large Flag blocks	7 strips	1½" wide
	Light Log Cabin block centers	2 strips	2½" wide
	Small and tall Boat blocks	12 rectangles	2½" x 6½"
	Large Boat blocks	3 rectangles	2½" x 12½"
Light red	Small Flag blocks	3 strips	1½" wide
	Light Log Cabin blocks	8 strips	1½" wide
Light blue	Light Log Cabin blocks	8 strips	1½" wide
	Plaid Log Cabin blocks	5 strips	1½" wide
	Large Flag block	1 strip	1½" wide
Red gingham	Plaid Log Cabin blocks and binding	7 strips	2½" wide
Red plaid	Plaid Log Cabin blocks	6 strips	1½" wide
Dark blue	Large and tall Boat blocks	4 strips	2½" wide
	Small and large Boat blocks	3 strips	2⅞" wide
	Large Boat blocks	3 rectangles	1½" x 12½"
	Tall Boat block	2 rectangles	1½" x 8½"
	Large and tall Boat blocks	1 strip	4½" wide
Light check	Small and large Boat blocks	3 strips	2⅞" wide
	Small Boat blocks	4 strips	2½" wide

Making the Small Flag Blocks

The small Flag blocks are half–Log Cabin blocks; strips are sewn to just 2 sides of the starting square. These blocks finish at 6" square.

1. From the 3½" dark blue plaid strip, cut 11 squares, 3½" x 3½".

2. Place a 1½" red strip on a 3½" blue plaid square, right sides together and raw edges aligned. Sew the strip to the square. Trim the strip even with the bottom of the square. Flip the red log open to the right and press.

3. Turn this unit to the left (counterclockwise) so that the log you just added is at the top of the unit. Sew another red strip to the right side of the unit; trim and press as above.

4. Turn the unit to the left (counterclockwise) and sew a light red strip to the first red log you attached. Trim and press. Sew a second light red strip to the second red log. Trim and press.

5. Turn the block to the left and repeat steps 2 and 3, this time adding 2 more red logs, to complete the block. Repeat to make a total of 11 small Flag blocks.

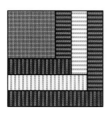

Small Flag Block
Make 11.

Making the Light Log Cabin Blocks

From the 2½" red strips, cut 18 squares, 2½" x 2½", for the centers of the light Log Cabin blocks. Referring to "Log Cabin Block Construction" on page 7, make 18 light Log Cabin blocks with the 2½" red squares and the 1½" light red and light blue strips for the logs. Begin piecing with the light blue logs.

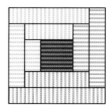

Light Log Cabin Block
Make 18.

Making the Plaid Log Cabin Blocks

From 1 of the 2½" red gingham strips, cut 11 squares, 2½" x 2½", for the plaid Log Cabin block centers. Referring to "Log Cabin Block Construction" on page 7, make 11 blocks with the 2½" red gingham squares and the 1½" red plaid and light blue strips for the logs. Begin piecing with the light blue logs.

Plaid Log Cabin Block
Make 11.

Making the Large Flag Block

1. From a 1½" red strip, cut 2 pieces, 1½" x 6½", and 1 piece, 1½" x 12½". Cut the same pieces from a light blue strip. Sew the 6½" pieces together along their long edges, alternating the red and light blue fabrics. Sew the 12½" red and blue strips together. Press the seam allowances toward the red strips.

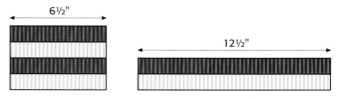

2. Sew the dark blue plaid 4½" x 6½" rectangle to the right edge of the 4½" x 6½" striped unit, sewing along the 4½" edge. Make sure the red strip is at the top of the unit. Press the seam allowance toward the blue fabric.

3. Sew the 12½" unit to the bottom of the unit from step 2. Make sure the red strip is joined to the dark blue rectangle. Press the seam allowance toward the red strip.

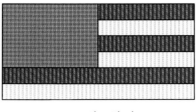

Large Flag Block
Make 1.

Making the Small Boat Blocks

1. Place the 2⅞" light check and dark blue strips right sides together in pairs. You should have 3 pairs. Press strips together and then carefully move them to your cutting mat. Cut 29 pairs of 2⅞" squares from the strips, making sure the pairs are lined up accurately before cutting.

2. Carefully draw a diagonal line from corner to corner on the light check squares, making sure you don't move the squares out of alignment.

3. Sew ¼" from the drawn line on both sides of the line; then cut the triangles apart on the drawn line. Press the seam allowances toward the dark fabric. Clip the tiny triangles or "dog ears" from the completed triangle squares. You'll need 58 triangle squares for the small Boat blocks. Reserve the remaining 25 triangle squares for the large Boat blocks.

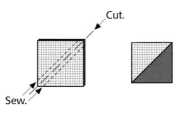

4. From the 2½" light check strips, cut 33 squares, 2½" x 2½". Draw a diagonal line on the wrong side of 22 of these squares. Also cut 11 light check rectangles, 2½" x 4½". (Reserve the rectangles and remaining 11 squares for step 5.) Place a 2½" light check square at either end of 11 of the 2½" x 6½" red rectangles. Sew along the marked lines, trim away the triangles below the stitching lines, and then press open the remaining triangles.

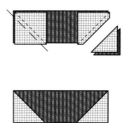

Small Boat Unit
Make 11.

5. To assemble the small Boat blocks, lay out a completed boat unit, 3 of the triangle squares made in step 3, a 2½" light check square, and a 2½" x 4½" light check rectangle, as shown. Sew the triangle squares and plain square together into a four-patch unit; then sew the light check rectangle to the right side of the four-patch unit. Sew the small boat unit to the bottom. Repeat to make 11 small Boat blocks.

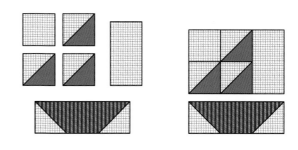

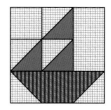

Small Boat Block
Make 11.

Making the Large and Tall Boat Blocks

1. From a 2½" dark blue strip, cut eight 2½" squares. Draw a diagonal line on the wrong side of each square. For the large boats, place the squares at both ends of the three 2½" x 12½" red rectangles. The tall boat is made from a 2½" x 6½" red rectangle, like the small boats, but with dark blue squares instead of light check squares.

2. Sew on the drawn lines, trim, and press as in step 4 of "Making the Small Boat Blocks." To complete the bottom of the large boats, sew a 1½" x 12½" dark blue rectangle to the bottom of the 3 large boat units. Be sure to catch the raw edges of the blue triangles in the seam.

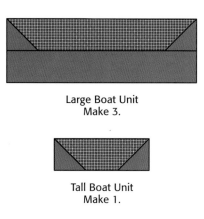

Large Boat Unit
Make 3.

Tall Boat Unit
Make 1.

3. From the 2½" and 4½" dark blue strips, cut the following pieces for steps 4–7:

    4 rectangles, 2½" x 6½"
    4 rectangles, 2½" x 4½"
    3 squares, 2½" x 2½"
    3 rectangles, 2½" x 12½"
    3 rectangles, 4½" x 6½"

4. The sail units for the large boats are made of 3 rows. For the top row, sew a triangle square from step 3 on page 37 to one end of a 2½" x 6½" dark blue rectangle. For the middle row, sew 2 triangle squares together and sew them to one 2½" x 4½" dark blue rectangle. For the bottom row, join 3 triangle squares and one 2½" dark blue square. Sew the rows together; then sew a 4½" x 6½" dark blue rectangle to the left side of the sail. Repeat to make a total of 3 sail units.

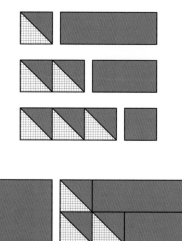

Make 3.

5. Sew the sail units to the top of the large boat units; then join a 2½" x 12½" dark blue strip to the top of the sails to complete 3 large Boat blocks.

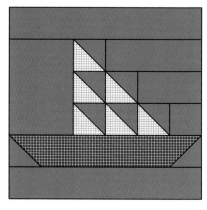

Large Boat Block
Make 3.

6. To make the sail for the tall boat, sew 4 triangle squares from step 3 on page 37 together in a four-patch unit. Join 2 more triangle squares, one on top of the other, as shown. Sew a 2½" x 4½" dark blue rectangle to the left side of the stacked triangle squares. Sew this unit to the top of the triangle square four-patch unit.

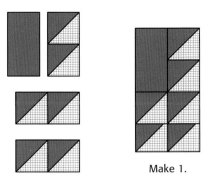

Make 1.

7. Sew one dark blue 1½" x 8½" strip to each side of the sail unit made in step 6. Join a 2½" x 6½" dark blue rectangle to the top of the sail unit; then sew the tall boat unit to the sail unit.

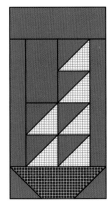

Tall Boat Block
Make 1.

Assembling the Quilt

Referring to the instructions in "Assembling and Quilting" on page 9 and the quilt layout below, construct your quilt top. While most blocks are 6", some are larger, so you'll need to assemble the units first, as shown. After the units are assembled, sew them together.

Quilt Layout

Finishing the Quilt

Follow the directions for quilting in "Assembling and Quilting" on page 9.

1. Piece the quilt backing; then layer the backing, batting, and quilt top; pin baste.

2. Quilt. I machine quilted through the center of each log and ¼" inside each triangle with invisible thread. I used large free-motion meandering on the boat backgrounds, the red boats, and the blue field of the large flag.

3. You may bind your quilt now or after the appliquilting is finished; see "Binding" on page 14. Use the 6 remaining 2½" red gingham strips for binding. Be sure to label your quilt.

Appliquilting

1. Referring to "Preparing the Appliqué Motifs" on page 11, and using the appliqué patterns below, cut and prepare 4 large stars, 16 medium stars, and 1 small star. Also prepare 3 large flags, 1 large flag reversed, and 11 small flags. All appliqué motifs are cut from the gold solid fabric.

2. Place the appliqués on the quilt, referring to the quilt photograph on page 34 for ideas.

3. Following the instructions in "Needle-Turn Appliquilt Stitch" on page 12, sew the motifs to the quilt with red topstitching thread.

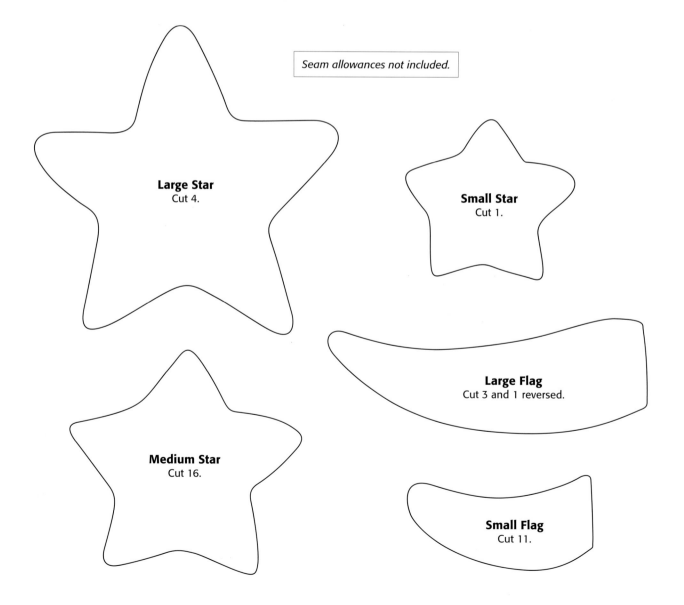

Seam allowances not included.

Large Star
Cut 4.

Small Star
Cut 1.

Medium Star
Cut 16.

Large Flag
Cut 3 and 1 reversed.

Small Flag
Cut 11.

THIS QUILT is a particular favorite of mine. I love all the subtle greens blended with just a touch of soft aqua. It's perfect for snuggling under in the last days of winter while you're dreaming of spring—no matter what colors you choose. Some of the assorted green plaids are cut slightly off kilter, which gives the Log Cabin patchwork a folk art flavor. The wide cream strips behind the vines both highlight the appliqué and make it easier to do since you don't have to stitch through so many seam allowances.

Finished quilt size: 47¾" x 63½"
Finished block size: 5¼" x 5¼"
Finished strip width: 5¼"

Materials

Yardages are based on 40"-wide fabric.

1⅝ yds. *total* of 3 assorted green plaids for blocks
1½ yds. *total* of 3 or 4 assorted beiges for block and appliqué background
1¼ yds. cream solid for appliqué background
⅞ yd. green stripe for vines, stems, and binding
½ yd. small green plaid for leaf appliqués
¼ yd. large green plaid for leaf appliqués
¼ yd. light green plaid for block centers
⅛ yd. or scraps of light green solid for leaf appliqués
⅛ yd. or scraps of light turquoise for flower appliqués

⅛ yd. or scraps of dark turquoise for flower appliqués
⅛ yd. or scraps of gold for flower appliqués
3 yds. fabric for backing
52" x 68" piece of batting

Making the Log Cabin Blocks

1. Sew a light green plaid strip for the block centers and a beige strip together along one long edge. Repeat to make a total of 3 strip sets. Press the seam allowances; then cut the strip sets into 72 segments, 1¼" wide.

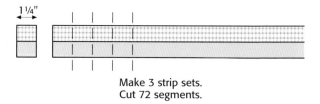

Make 3 strip sets.
Cut 72 segments.

2. Using the 1¼" assorted beige and assorted green plaid strips, continue piecing the Log Cabin blocks, referring to "Log Cabin Block Construction" on page 7. Each block has 3 rounds. Half of each round is made of beige logs, half of green plaid logs.

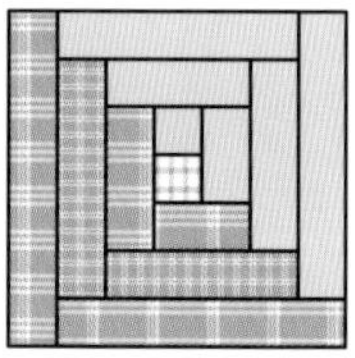

Log Cabin Block
Make 72.

Cutting

All fabric strips are cut across the grain of the fabric, except where noted. All cut sizes allow for ¼" seam allowances.

Fabric	Used For	Number to Cut	Size to Cut
Light green plaid	Block centers	3 strips	1¼" wide
Assorted beiges	Blocks	39 strips	1¼" wide
	Appliqué background	3 squares	5¾" x 5¾"
Assorted green plaids	Blocks	41 strips	1¼" wide
Cream solid	Appliqué background	6 lengthwise strips	5¾" wide
Green stripe	Vines*	5 strips	1" wide
	Stems*	1 strip	¾" wide
	Binding	6 strips	2½" wide

Typically, vines and stems for appliqué are cut on the bias to make them more pliable on curves, but flannels and homespuns are flexible enough to make gentle curves even when cut on the crossgrain of the fabric.

Assembling the Quilt

1. Following the quilt layout below, sew the blocks into 6 rows, with 12 blocks in each row. Press the seam allowances to one side.

2. From the six 5¾" cream solid strips, cut the following pieces:

Number to Cut	Length to Cut
2	16¼"
2	42½"
1	26¾"
1	32"

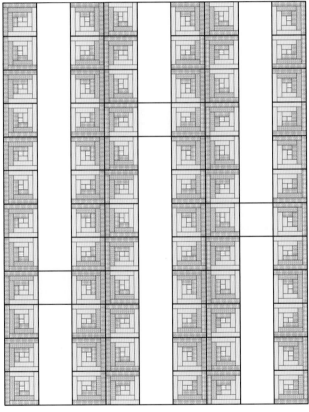

Quilt Layout

3. For the left and center appliqué strips, sew a 5¾" beige square between a 16¼" and a 42½" cream strip. For the right appliqué strip, sew a 5¾" beige square between the 26¾" and the 32" cream strips. Press the seams to one side.

4. Sew the 3 appliqué strips between the rows of Log Cabin blocks. Press the seams toward the blocks. Double-check placement before

sewing, to make sure the green portions of the blocks create an undulating pattern that nicely echoes the appliquéd vines.

Finishing the Quilt

Follow the directions for quilting in "Assembling and Quilting" on page 9.

1. Piece the quilt backing; then layer the backing, batting, and quilt top; pin baste.

2. Hand or machine quilt to stabilize the layers. I quilted in the ditch around each Log Cabin block with white thread.

3. You may bind your quilt now or after the appliquilting is finished; see "Binding" on page 14.

Appliquilting

1. Referring to "Preparing the Appliqué Motifs" on page 11 and using the appliqué patterns on page 44, cut and prepare 50 to 55 *each* of the medium and large leaves and 18 to 20 small leaves from the small and large green plaids. Also make 13 flowers (13 center petals, 26 outer petals, and 13 flower centers). The center petals are dark turquoise, the outer petals are light turquoise, and the flower centers are gold.

2. Refer to the quilt photograph on page 41 as a guide or use your own creativity to arrange the vines, leaves, and stems. Referring to "Vines and Stems" on page 13, make the vines from the 1" green stripe strips. Make the stems from the ¾" green stripe strips. Rather than sewing the 1" strips together to make one long strip, cut 3 of the 40" strips in half and overlay a 20" length near the end of each 40" strip. Pin the appliqués in place.

3. Following the instructions in "Needle-Turn Appliquilt Stitch" on page 12, sew the motifs to your quilt with linen thread, or substitute ecru topstitching thread or embroidery floss.

4. Be sure to label your quilt, and add a hanging sleeve if desired.

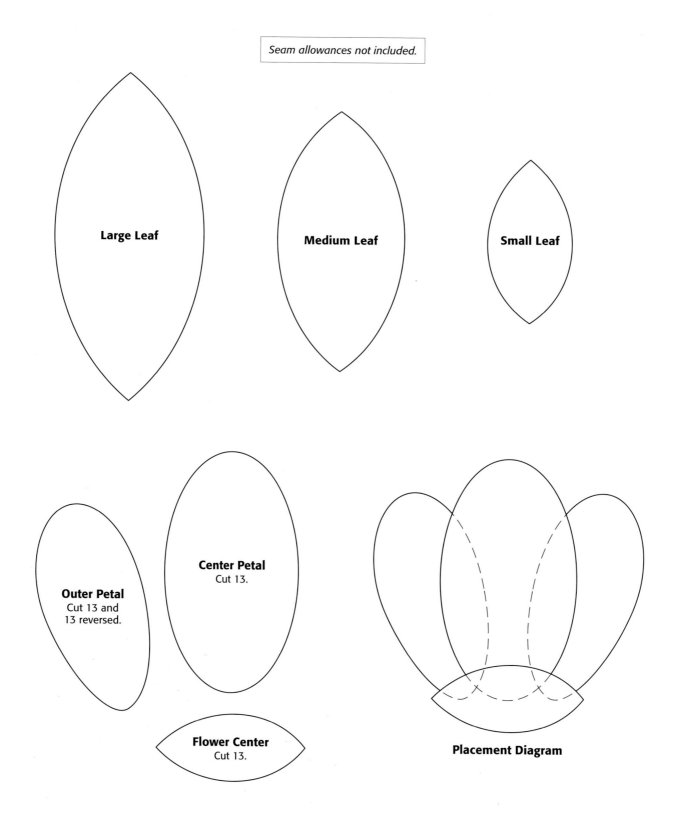

Seam allowances not included.

Large Leaf

Medium Leaf

Small Leaf

Outer Petal
Cut 13 and
13 reversed.

Center Petal
Cut 13.

Flower Center
Cut 13.

Placement Diagram

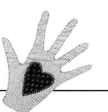

YOU MAY think of Valentine's Day when you see this quilt, but hearts are appropriate year-round and can be any color you wish. Imagine this pattern in a rich palette of blues, greens, tans, golds, reds, and purples. Or picture it in a mix of soft pastels. In this true red version, a few hints of gold add a bit of sparkle.

Finished quilt size: 49½" x 63½"
Finished block size: 7" x 7"

Materials

Yardages are based on 40"-wide fabric.

1⅝ yds. *total* of assorted light reds for blocks
1¾ yds. *total* of assorted dark reds for blocks
½ yd. red check for block centers
¼ yd. white solid for hand and heart appliqués
¼ yd. red solid for heart appliqués
3 yds. fabric for backing
⅝ yd. red-and-white stripe for binding
54" x 68" piece of batting

Making the Log Cabin Blocks

All the Log Cabin blocks in this quilt are identical. Following instructions in "Log Cabin Block Construction" on page 7 and the directions below, make 43 blocks.

1. Sew the 3" red check strips to 1¼" light red strips. Make 4 strip sets. Cut the strip sets into 43 units, each 3" long. These units are the Log Cabin block centers and the first logs.

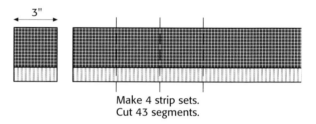

Make 4 strip sets.
Cut 43 segments.

2. Using the light red strips and dark red strips, continue joining logs around the block centers until each block has 3 rounds of logs. They should measure 7½" with seam allowances.

Log Cabin Block
Make 43.

Cutting

All fabric strips are cut across the grain of the fabric. All cut sizes allow for ¼" seam allowances.

Fabric	Used For	Number to Cut	Size to Cut
Red check	Block centers	4 strips	3" wide
Light reds	Blocks	25 strips	1¼" wide
	Appliqué background	2 squares	7½" x 7½"
	Appliqué background	2 rectangles	7½" x 14½"
Dark reds	Blocks	37 strips	1¼" wide
	Appliqué background	5 squares	7½" x 7½"
	Appliqué background	1 square	14½" x 14½"
	Appliqué background	1 rectangle	7½" x 21½"
Red-and-white stripe	Binding	6 strips	2½" wide

Assembling the Quilt

Following the quilt layout below, sew the Log Cabin blocks, light red and dark red 7½" squares, and appliqué background rectangles together. Sew the blocks and backgrounds together in units rather than rows before assembling the entire quilt.

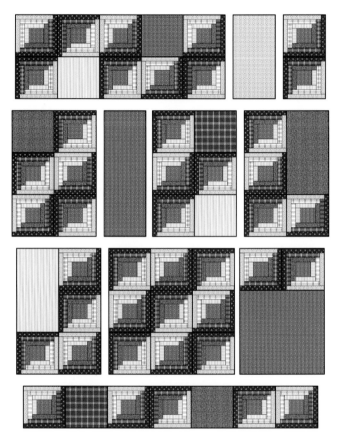

Quilt Layout

Finishing the Quilt

Follow the directions for quilting in "Assembling and Quilting" on page 9.

1. Piece the quilt backing; then layer the backing, batting, and quilt top; pin baste.

2. Quilt. I machine quilted through the middle of each log. After appliquilting the heart motifs on the plain squares and rectangles, I echo quilted by machine around each design.

3. You may bind your quilt now or after the appliquilting is finished; see "Binding" on page 14. If you don't bind your quilt before appliquilting, I recommend basting around the edges before you appliquilt because some of the larger backgrounds are along the edge of the quilt. Be sure to label your quilt.

Appliquilting

1. Referring to "Preparing the Appliqué Motifs" on page 11 and using the appliqué patterns on pages 48–52, cut and prepare the various heart motifs and large hand motif.

2. Refer to the quilt photograph on page 45 as a guide or use your own creativity to arrange the motifs as you wish. For example, you may want to use your own or a family member's handprint in place of the pattern given. The quilt shown has a small heart appliquilted to the center of each Log Cabin block. The hand is appliquilted in the large red square, and the long hearts are appliquilted in the rectangles. Five small hearts combine to make a flower design in one of the 7" blocks.

3. Appliquilt the heart and hand motifs, referring to "Needle-Turn Appliquilt Stitch" on page 12. After stitching the large hearts, quilt the backgrounds with a meandering stitch, or outline them either by hand or machine.

4. The solid white heart on the red print 7" square in the bottom row is reverse appliquéd. To do this, trace around the smaller heart template in the center of the larger heart (page 48). Cut away the inside of the smaller heart ¼" inside the drawn line. Clip the curves of the small heart and turn the seam allowance under on the drawn line as you stitch. The red background fabric will be exposed, making a white heart surrounding a red heart.

5. The larger hearts are decorated with smaller appliquéd hearts, running stitches, or other embroidery. The Xs on the patterns are 2 straight stitches, one over the other. The Xs and running stitch are done with 3 strands of embroidery floss. Embroider through all the quilt layers so the large areas are quilted.

6. Bind your quilt if you did not do so earlier, and add a hanging sleeve if desired.

Seam allowances not included.

Placement Diagrams

Seam allowances not included.

Connect to pattern on page 50.

Connect to pattern on page 49.

Seam allowances not included.

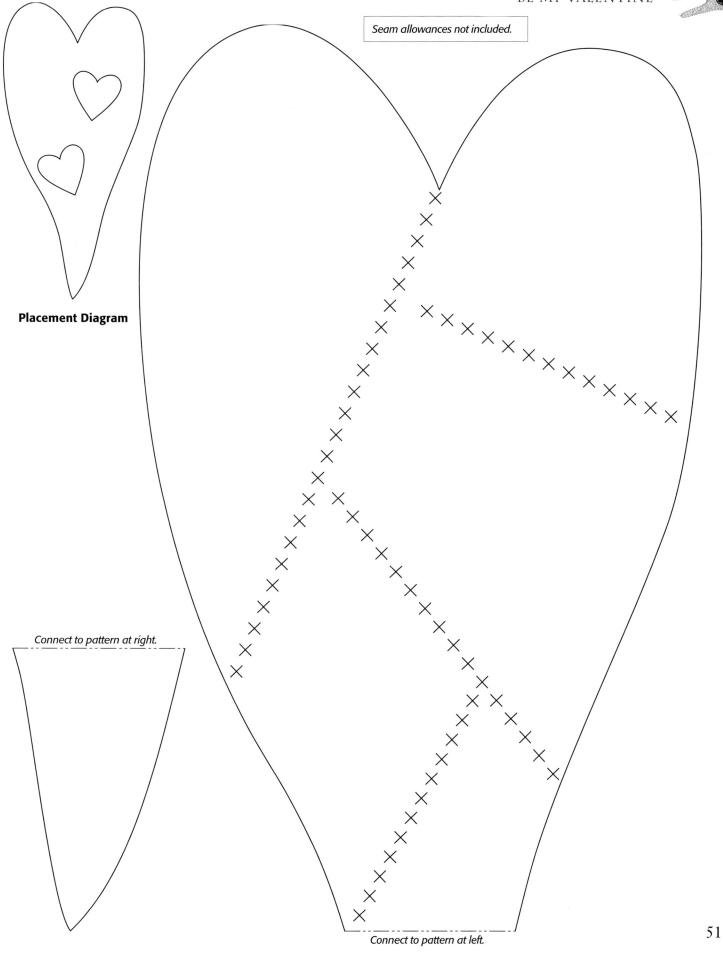

Seam allowances not included.

Placement Diagram

Connect to pattern at right.

Connect to pattern at left.

Seam allowances not included.

DEEP REDS and olive greens, a Barn Raising setting, and traditional appliqué all lend a classic air to this quilt. But the off-center set and borders on just two sides also give it a touch of contemporary whimsy.

Perfect for a den or family room, this quilt is sure to be enjoyed by all who are lucky enough to snuggle under it. And the appliqués are easy to stitch with their gently curving shapes.

Finished quilt size: 63½" x 63½"
Finished block size: 7" x 7"

Materials

Yardages are based on 40"-wide fabric.

3 yds. assorted lights for blocks and border
2⅝ yds. assorted darks for blocks
1 yd. green for leaf, frond, and sepal appliqués
¾ yd. red for block centers, posy appliqués, and flower appliqués
⅜ yd. gold for posy and flower center appliqués
3⅞ yds. fabric for backing
⅝ yd. fabric for binding
68" x 68" piece of batting

Cutting

All fabric strips are cut across the grain of the fabric. All cut sizes allow for ¼" seam allowances.

Fabric	Used For	Number to Cut	Size to Cut
Red	Block centers	3 strips	1½" wide
Assorted lights	Log Cabin blocks	25 strips	1½" wide
	Courthouse Steps blocks	5 strips	1½" wide
	Border	4 strips	7½" x 21½"
	Center background	1 square	14½" x 14½"
Assorted darks	Log Cabin blocks	27 strips	1½" wide
	Courthouse Steps blocks	3 strips	1½" wide
Binding fabric	Binding	7 strips	2½" wide

Making the Log Cabin Blocks

Referring to "Log Cabin Block Construction" on page 7, make 64 blocks. All blocks start with a red strip for the center, and logs start with the assorted light fabrics followed by the assorted dark fabrics. Each block has 3 rounds.

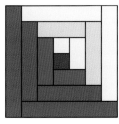

Log Cabin Block
Make 64.

Making the Courthouse Steps Blocks

Courthouse Steps blocks are a Log Cabin variation. Rather than sewing the strips to the center unit in a counterclockwise manner, sew logs on opposite sides of the center; then turn the center and sew logs on the other 2 sides.

1. Cut a 1½" red strip and a 1½" light strip in half so they're each about 20" long. Sew the red half strip and the light half strip together lengthwise. Sew the remaining half of the light strip to the opposite side of the red strip. Press the seam allowances; then cut the strip set into 1½" units. You'll need 5 segments.

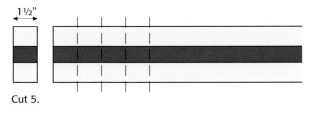

1½"

Cut 5.

2. Join a 1½" dark strip to the center units, sewing the strip to the 3½" long end of the center unit. Trim the strip even with the center unit; then sew the remaining red strip to the opposite side of the block.

3½"

3. Turn the block and add light strips to the sides opposite the dark strips added in step 2. This completes 1 round. Continue building the block around the center unit, sewing logs to opposite sides of the block rather than attaching them in a counterclockwise manner. Make a total of 5 Courthouse Steps blocks, each with 3 rounds of logs.

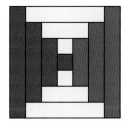

Courthouse Steps Block
Make 5.

Assembling the Quilt

1. Following the quilt plan on page 56, sew the Log Cabin blocks into 8 rows of 8 blocks each. Note that a 14½" light square is used in place of 4 Log Cabin blocks in rows 3 and 4. Join the blocks in these rows to the light squares before sewing the rows together.

2. For the side and bottom borders, sew a Courthouse Steps block between 2 of the 7½" x 21½" light strips. Make sure you sew the light sides of the blocks to the light strips.

3. Sew a Courthouse Steps block to the end of one of the borders constructed in step 2. Sew this border to the left side of the quilt center, referring to the quilt plan on page 56. Press the seam allowances toward the center of the quilt top.

4. Sew the remaining Courthouse Steps blocks at each end of the other border. Press the seams toward the rectangles.

5. Sew the border to the bottom of the quilt, referring to the quilt plan below. Press the seams toward the center of the quilt

Quilt Plan

Finishing the Quilt

Follow the directions for quilting in "Assembling and Quilting" on page 9.

1. Piece the quilt backing; then layer the backing, batting, and quilt top; pin baste.

2. Quilt. I machine quilted through the center of each log with monofilament in the machine needle and cotton thread in the bobbin. If you'll be hand quilting, match the thread to the log fabrics.

3. For this quilt, I recommend waiting to bind your quilt until after the appliqué flowers have been added to the borders. Otherwise, you'll be adding binding to an unquilted border.

Appliquilting

1. Referring to "Preparing the Appliqué Motifs" on page 11 and using the appliqué patterns on pages 57–59, cut and prepare the posy, flower, leaf, and frond motifs. The posies and flowers are cut from red fabric; the leaves, fronds, and sepals from green fabric; and the posy and flower centers from gold fabric. In the border, there are 24 large posies with leaf and stem units. In the interior of the quilt, there are 20 flowers, 3 flowers with sepals, 9 small posies, and 4 small posies with leaves.

You will also need to cut 4 center fronds, four 8" fronds, two 11" fronds, and one 17" frond for the light areas of the quilt. Except for the center fronds, you will need to trace the pattern, then flip it over and trace the other half of the pattern, as indicated on the pattern pages.

You may stitch the small gold flower centers to the red flowers before stitching the flowers to the quilt, as well as the gold centers to the small and large red circles of the posies.

2. Refer to the photo on page 53 for placement of flowers and leaves on light areas of the blocks. Pin motifs in place. Following directions in "Needle-Turn Appliquilt Stitch" on page 12, stitch the motifs in place.

3. Bind your quilt, referring to "Binding" on page 14.

4. Be sure to label your quilt.

Seam allowances not included.

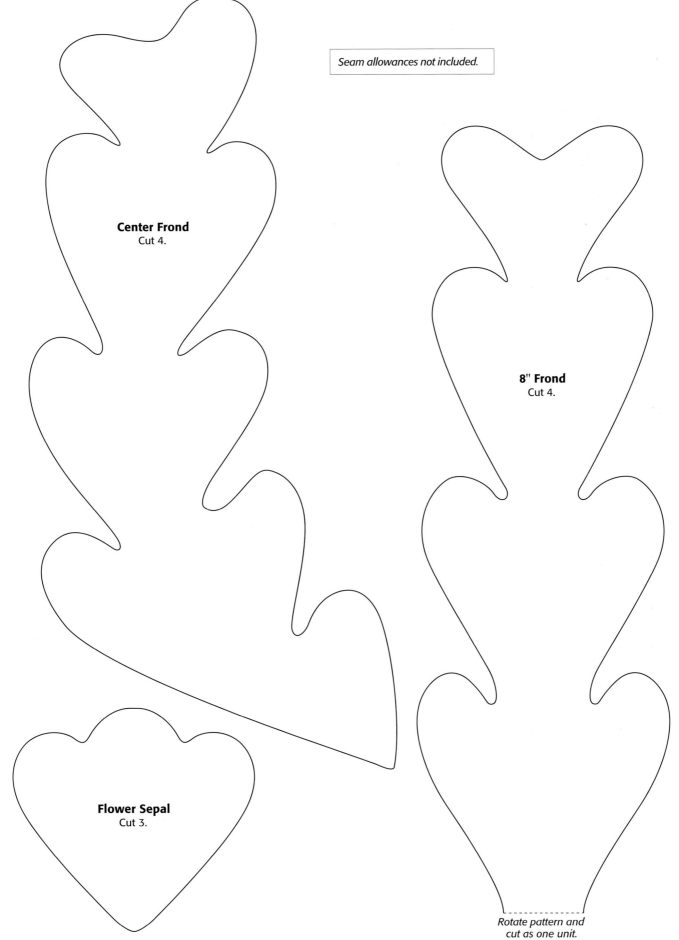

Center Frond
Cut 4.

8" Frond
Cut 4.

Flower Sepal
Cut 3.

*Rotate pattern and
cut as one unit.*

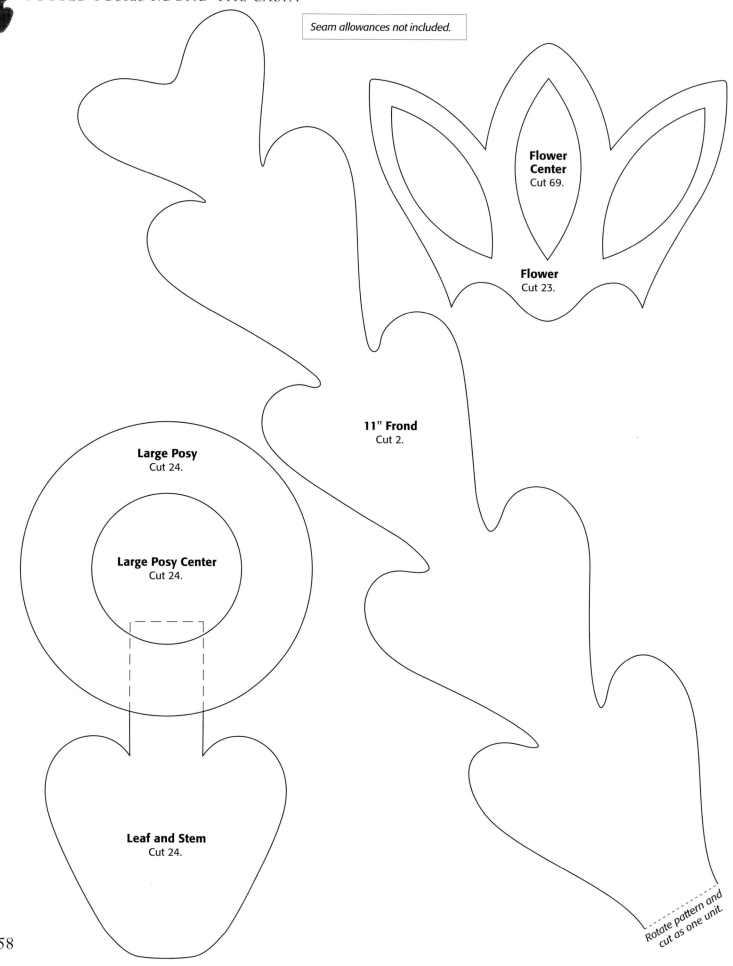

Seam allowances not included.

Flower Center
Cut 69.

Flower
Cut 23.

11" Frond
Cut 2.

Large Posy
Cut 24.

Large Posy Center
Cut 24.

Leaf and Stem
Cut 24.

Rotate pattern and cut as one unit.

Seam allowances not included.

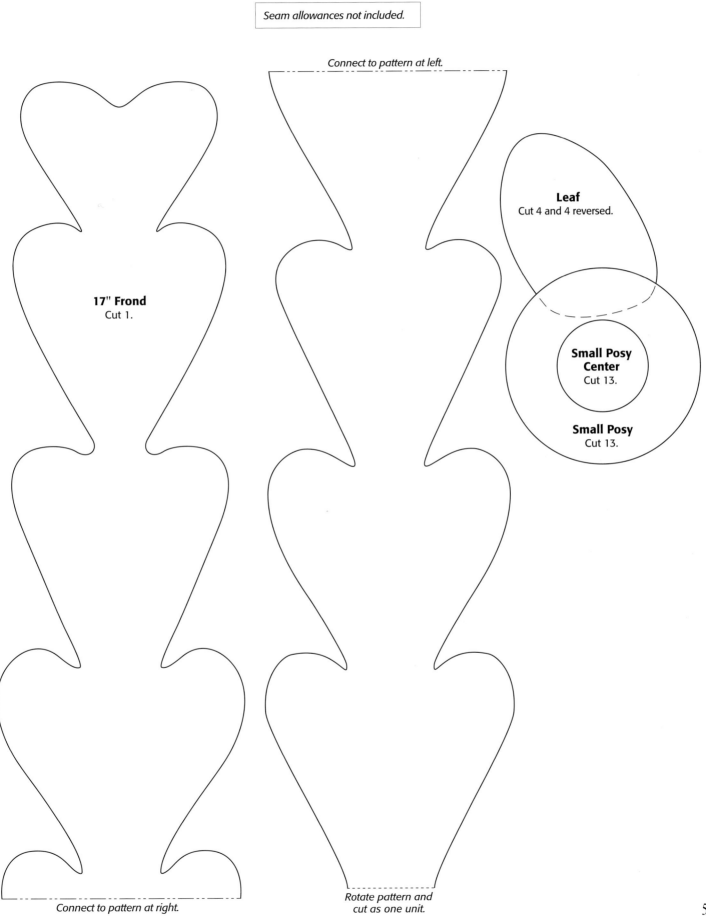

Connect to pattern at left.

Connect to pattern at right.

17" Frond
Cut 1.

Leaf
Cut 4 and 4 reversed.

Small Posy Center
Cut 13.

Small Posy
Cut 13.

Rotate pattern and
cut as one unit.

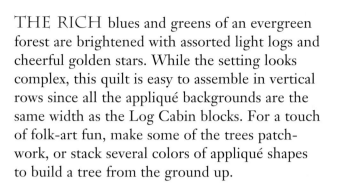

THE RICH blues and greens of an evergreen forest are brightened with assorted light logs and cheerful golden stars. While the setting looks complex, this quilt is easy to assemble in vertical rows since all the appliqué backgrounds are the same width as the Log Cabin blocks. For a touch of folk-art fun, make some of the trees patchwork, or stack several colors of appliqué shapes to build a tree from the ground up.

Finished quilt size: 57¾" x 63½"
Finished block size: 5¼" x 5¼"

Materials

Yardages are based on 40"-wide fabric.

1⅛ yds. dark blue solid for block centers, tree backgrounds, and border

1 yd. medium blue solid for tree backgrounds and border

½ yd. *each* of 3 assorted greens for blocks, tree appliqués, and border

½ yd. gold solid for star appliqués

⅜ yd. *each* of 3 assorted lights for blocks and border

¼ yd. brown for tree trunk appliqués

3⅜ yds. fabric for backing

⅝ yd. green print for binding

59" x 64" piece of batting

Making the Log Cabin Blocks

Referring to "Log Cabin Block Construction" on page 7, make 38 blocks.

1. All blocks start with a 1¼" dark blue solid strip for the center and a 1¼" light strip for the logs. Make 2 strip sets, and cut them into 1¼" segments.

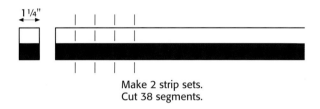

1¼"

Make 2 strip sets.
Cut 38 segments.

2. Turn the center units a quarter turn counterclockwise and add another light log. Repeat, adding 2 logs from the assorted greens to each block. Repeat so that each block has a total of 3 rounds, half light and half green. The blocks should measure 5¾".

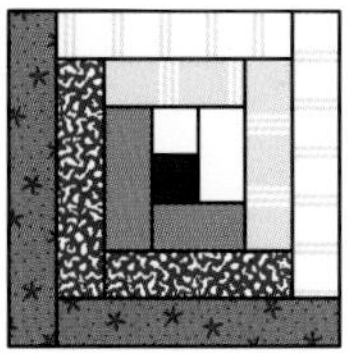

Log Cabin Block
Make 38.

Cutting

All fabric strips are cut across the grain of the fabric. All cut sizes allow for ¼" seam allowances.

Fabric	Used For	Number to Cut	Size to Cut
Dark blue solid	Block centers	2 strips	1¼" wide
	Tree backgrounds and border corners	5 strips	5¾" wide
	Border rectangles	3 strips	3" wide
Assorted lights	Blocks	18 strips	1¼" wide
	Border rectangles	3 strips	3" wide
Assorted greens	Blocks	23 strips	1¼" wide
	Border rectangles	5 strips	3" wide
Medium blue solid	Tree backgrounds and border corners	4 strips	5¾" wide
	Border rectangles	3 strips	3" wide
Green print	Binding	7 strips	2½" wide

Assembling the Quilt

The blocks in this quilt are set in a Straight Furrows pattern and intermingled with blocks appliquéd with trees. Before assembling the quilt, cut the dark and medium blue strips for tree backgrounds to the lengths indicated below.

From the 5¾" dark blue strips, cut:
1 rectangle, 5¾" x 21½"
3 rectangles, 5¾" x 16¼"
6 rectangles, 5¾" x 11"
4 squares, 5¾" x 5¾"

From the 5¾" medium blue strips, cut:
3 rectangles, 5¾" x 16¼"
6 rectangles, 5¾" x 11"
5 squares, 5¾" x 5¾"

1. Following the quilt layout below, lay out the Log Cabin blocks and dark and medium blue rectangles and squares. Sew the pieces together in vertical rows. Press the seams in opposite directions from one row to another. Sew the rows together and press the quilt top.

2. Assemble all the 3" border strips (assorted lights, assorted greens, dark blue, and medium blue). Cut the strips into 3" x 5¾" rectangles. Sew the rectangles together randomly along their 5¾" edges. Make 4 borders, 2 with 19 rectangles each and 2 with 21 rectangles each.

3. Sew the 2 shorter borders to opposite sides of the quilt. Press the seam allowances toward the quilt center.

4. Sew a 5¾" dark blue square to one end and a 5¾" medium blue square to the opposite end of the 2 longer borders. Press the seams toward the corner squares. Sew these borders to the top and bottom of the quilt; press.

Finishing the Quilt

Follow the directions for quilting in "Assembling and Quilting" on page 9.

1. Piece the quilt backing, and then layer the backing, batting, and quilt top; pin baste.

Quilt Layout

2. Quilt. I machine quilted the logs lengthwise through the middle and quilted the border in vertical straight lines spaced 1" apart. I used gold quilting thread to coordinate with the gold star appliqués.

3. You may bind your quilt now or after the appliquilting is finished; see "Binding" on page 14.

Appliquilting

1. Referring to "Preparing the Appliqué Motifs" on page 11 and using the appliqué patterns at right and on pages 64–68, cut and prepare the motifs using various greens for the trees, brown for the tree trunks, and gold for the stars.

2. Referring to the quilt photo on page 60 for placement, pin the motifs in place. Some of the trees are appliquéd in several different fabrics; arrange the pieces following the numerical order provided on the appliqué pattern. Other trees are pieced for a patch-work look.

3. Following the directions in "Needle-Turn Appliquilt Stitch" on page 12, stitch the motifs in place. The stars on the quilt shown are stitched with navy thread and the trees and trunks with gold thread. I also used gold thread to add cross-stitch details on the pieced tree seam lines.

4. After appliquilting the motifs, you may want to do some free-motion meander quilting in the backgrounds of the trees. This step is optional.

5. Bind your quilt if you did not do so earlier. Be sure to label your quilt.

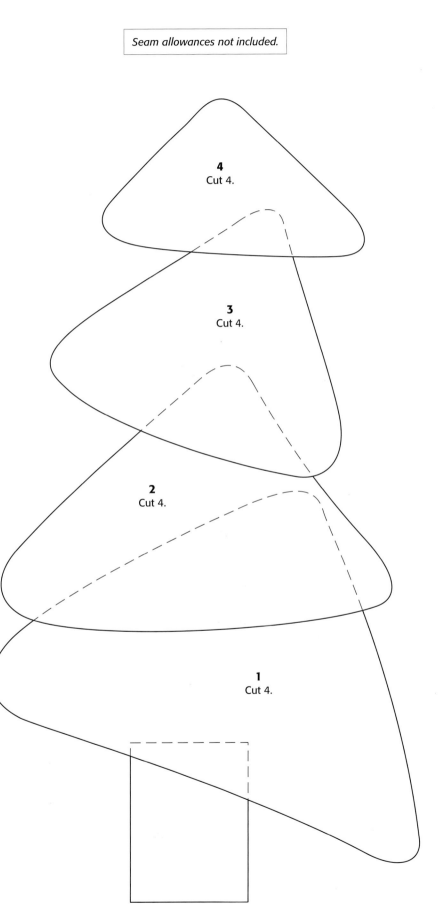

Seam allowances not included.

4
Cut 4.

3
Cut 4.

2
Cut 4.

1
Cut 4.

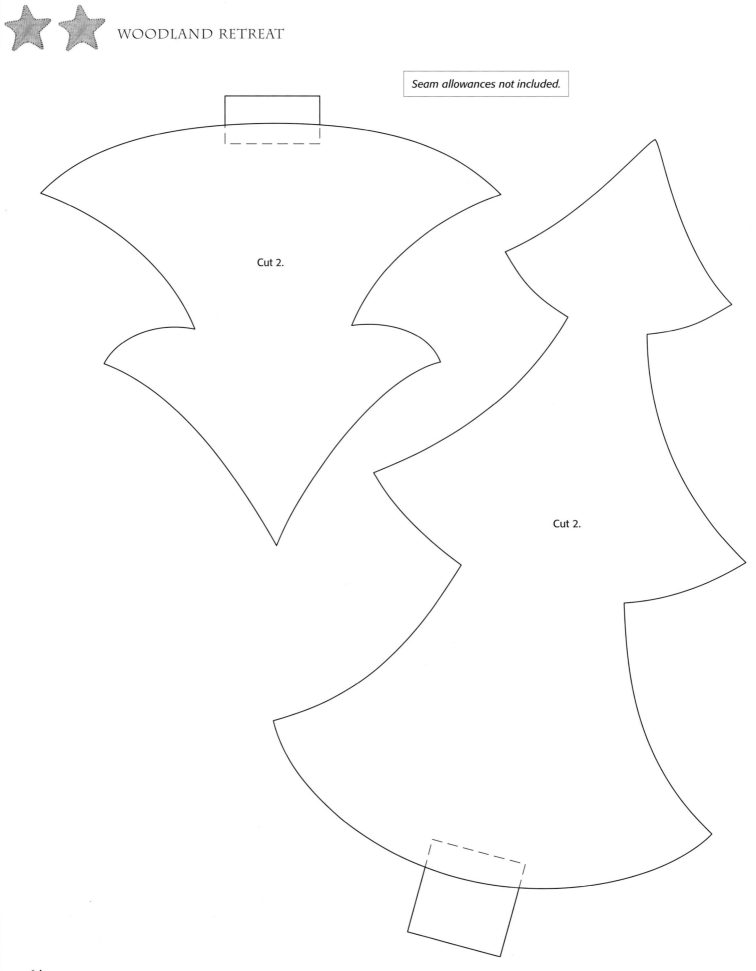

Seam allowances not included.

Cut 2.

Cut 2.

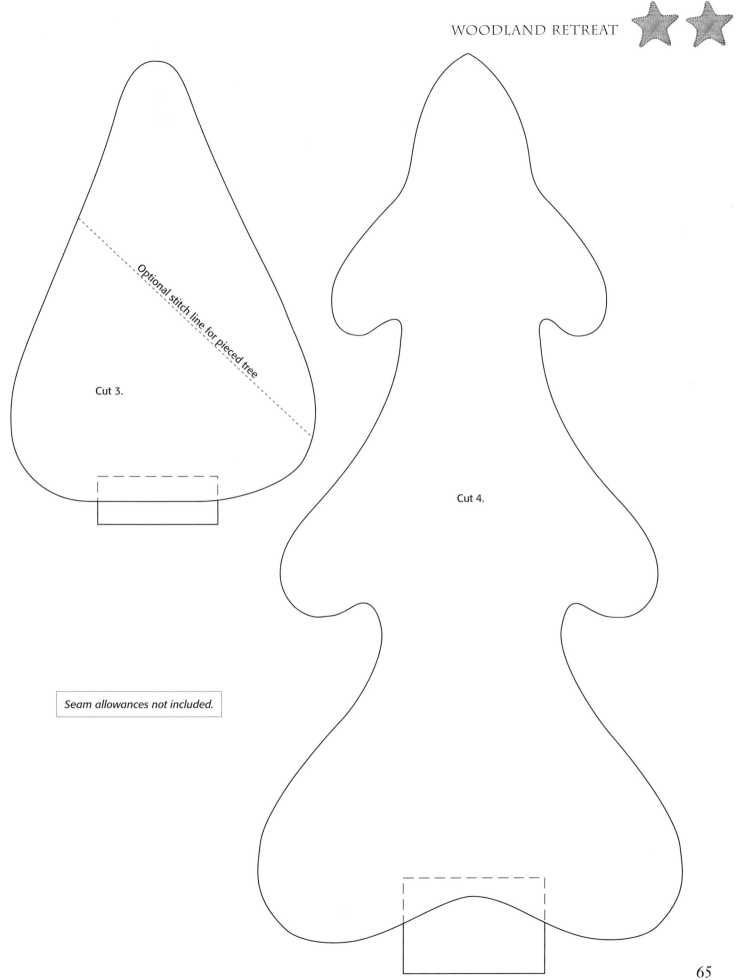

Optional stitch line for pieced tree

Cut 3.

Cut 4.

Seam allowances not included.

Enlarge patterns 200 percent.
Seam allowances not included.

Cut 3.

Cut 1.

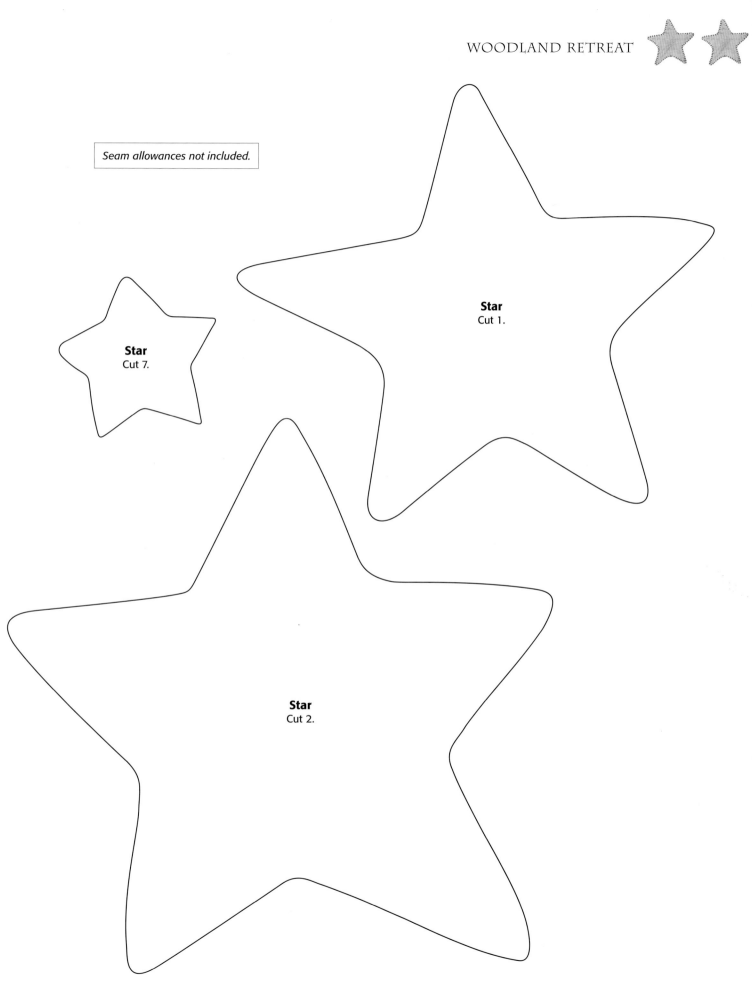

Seam allowances not included.

Star
Cut 7.

Star
Cut 1.

Star
Cut 2.

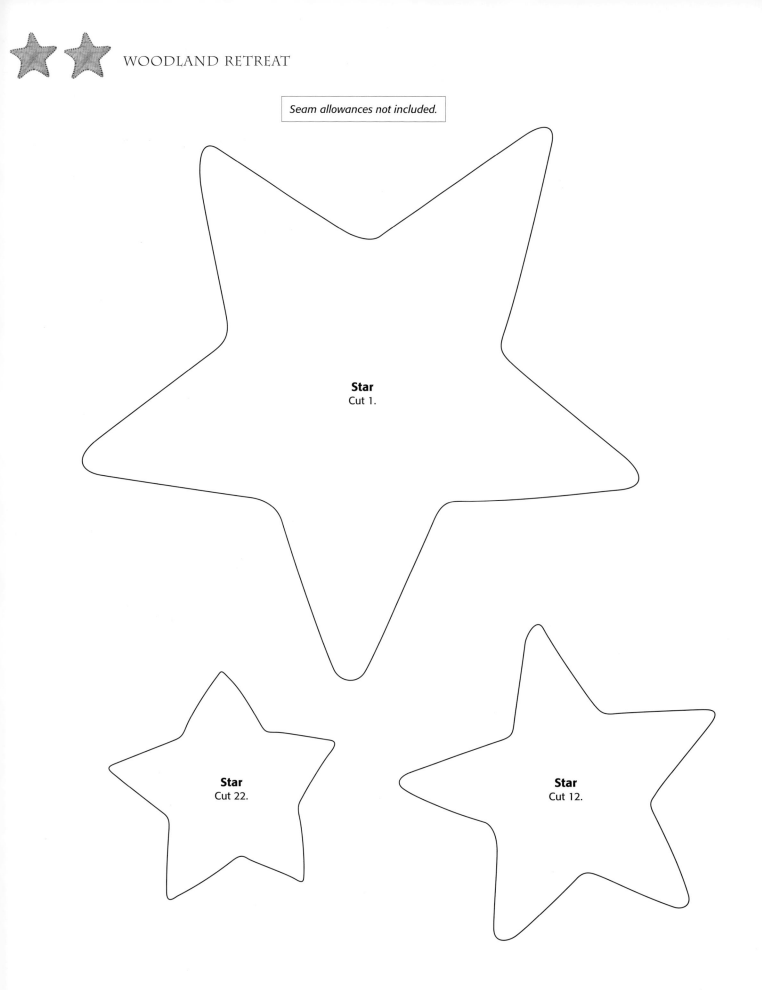

Seam allowances not included.

Star
Cut 1.

Star
Cut 22.

Star
Cut 12.

LET YOUR patriotic feelings show with this all-American quilt. The red and blue Log Cabin blocks are set on point in a flag configuration and highlighted with another traditional American symbol, the bald eagle. While there are fifty-one Log Cabin blocks in this quilt, notice that each contains only two rounds of logs, not three (as in the other projects in this book), so stitching the blocks can be quite speedy.

Finished quilt size: 44" x 57"
Finished block size: 3¾"

Materials

Yardages are based on 40"-wide fabric.

1½ yds. blue plaid for outer border
1⅜ yds. white for blocks, setting triangles, and eagle appliqué
1 yd. red for blocks and setting triangles
1 yd. dark blue solid for inner border, letter appliqués, and binding
¾ yd. blue for blocks and setting triangles
½ yd. red stripe for circle and letter appliqués
½ yd. gold for star appliqués
¼ yd. gray for eagle appliqué
2⅔ yds. fabric for backing
48" x 61" piece of batting

Cutting

All fabric strips are cut across the grain of the fabric, except where noted. All cut sizes allow for ¼" seam allowances.

Fabric	Used For	Number to Cut	Size to Cut
White	Blocks	16 strips	1¼" wide
	Setting triangles	2 squares	6⅝" x 6⅝"
		4 squares	3½" x 3½"
Blue	Blocks	8 strips	1¼" wide
	Setting triangles	3 squares	6⅝" x 6⅝"
		1 square	3½" x 3½"
Red	Blocks	9 strips	1¼" wide
	Setting triangles	3 squares	6⅝" x 6⅝"
		5 squares	3½" x 3½"
Dark blue solid	Inner border	4 strips	1½" wide
	Binding	6 strips	2½" wide
Blue plaid	Top outer border	1 lengthwise strip	10½" x 42¼"
	Bottom outer border	1 lengthwise strip	8½" x 42¼"
	Side outer borders	2 lengthwise strips	8½" x 44½"

Making the Log Cabin Blocks

1. Referring to "Log Cabin Block Construction" on page 7, make 12 Log Cabin blocks by using a 1¼" white strip for the block centers and 1¼" blue strips for the logs. Note that these blocks have only 2 rounds of logs, and that all logs are blue.

Log Cabin Block
Make 12.

2. In the same manner, make 39 Log Cabin blocks by using the 1¼" white strips for the block centers and 1¼" red strips and 1¼" white strips for the logs. Add the logs, beginning with the red strips and ending with the white strips. Again, these blocks have only 2 rounds of logs, not 3.

Log Cabin Block
Make 39.

Assembling the Quilt

1. Cut the three 6⅝" red squares in half diagonally twice to make 12 side setting triangles. You'll need only 10. In the same manner, cut the three 6⅝" blue squares and the two 6⅝" white squares in half diagonally twice. You'll need 10 blue triangles and 3 white ones.

2. Cut the 3½" red squares in half diagonally once to make 10 setting triangles. Repeat, cutting one 3½" blue square and four 3½" white squares in half diagonally once to make 2 triangles each.

3. Sew the red and white 3½" triangles together in pairs as shown to make larger triangle units. Make 5 units with the red triangles on the left, and 2 units with the red triangles on the right. In the same manner, sew a red and a blue triangle together, with the red triangle on the left. Sew a blue and a white triangle together, with the blue triangle on the left. You should have 2 red triangles left over for the top right and bottom left quilt corners.

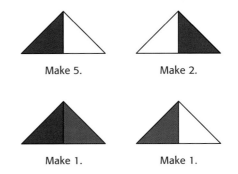

Make 5.   Make 2.

Make 1.   Make 1.

4. Before you can assemble the quilt in diagonal rows, you'll need to sew some of the triangles together to make blocks. Sew the 2 red-and-white triangle units with the white triangles on the left (from step 3) to 2 large blue triangles (from step 1). Also sew a large white triangle to a large blue triangle (from step 1); make 3.

Make 2.   Make 3.

5. Referring to the instructions in "Assembling and Quilting" on page 9 and the quilt layout below, construct the quilt top. Sew the Log Cabin blocks and side setting triangles into diagonal rows. I suggest that you sew entire rows; then lay out the rows on your design wall, floor, or table to prevent mistakes. Sew the rows together.

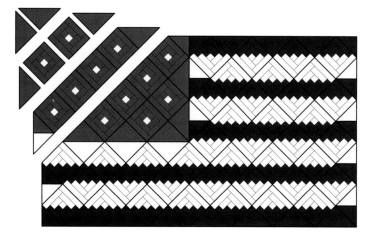

Quilt Layout

Adding the Border

1. Measure the quilt top through the horizontal center. Trim 2 of the 1½" dark blue inner border strips to this length. Pin the border strips to the top and bottom of the quilt top, matching the centers and ends. You may have to ease or stretch the border strips slightly to fit both edges, but it is important that the borders on opposite sides of the quilt are equal in length so that the quilt will lie flat. Sew the border strips to the quilt and press the seam allowances toward the borders.

2. In the same manner, measure the quilt top through the vertical center. Trim the remaining 1½" dark blue inner border strips to this length and sew the strips to the sides of the quilt top. Press the seam allowances toward the borders.

3. Measure the width of the quilt top, including the inner borders, and trim the 10½" x 42¼" blue plaid outer border strip to this length. Sew it to the top of the quilt, matching the centers and ends. Trim the 8½" x 42¼" outer border strip to the same length and sew it to the bottom of the quilt.

4. Measure the length of the quilt top, including the inner borders. Trim the remaining 8½" outer border strips to this length and sew them to the sides of the quilt top. Press the seam allowances toward the outer border.

Finishing the Quilt

Follow the directions for quilting in "Assembling and Quilting" on page 9.

1. Piece the quilt backing, and then layer the backing, batting, and quilt top; pin baste.

2. Quilt. In this project, I quilted wavy lines across the red and white stripes formed by the Log Cabin blocks set on point, rather than quilting through the center of each log as in other projects. In the blue areas, I used a meandering pattern.

3. You may bind your quilt now or after the appliquilting is finished; see "Binding" on page 14. Use the 2½" dark blue strips for binding.

Appliquilting

1. Referring to "Preparing the Appliqué Motifs" on page 11 and using the appliqué patterns on pages 73–78, cut and prepare 8 large circles and 1 small circle for the star backgrounds from the red stripe fabric; 8 large stars and 1 small star from the gold fabric; 1 eagle head and tail from the white fabric; and 1 eagle body, 1 wing, and 1 wing reversed from the gray fabric. Also prepare the "God Bless" and "ll" from the dark blue fabric, and the "US" and "A" from the red stripe fabric.

2. Referring to the photograph on page 69, place the motifs on the borders and pin in place.

3. Following the instructions in "Needle-Turn Appliquilt Stitch" on page 12, sew the motifs to the quilt using red topstitching thread. To emphasize the gold stars on the red circles, I made long running stitches in red thread inside the appliquilt stitches.

4. Bind your quilt if you did not do so earlier. Be sure to label your quilt.

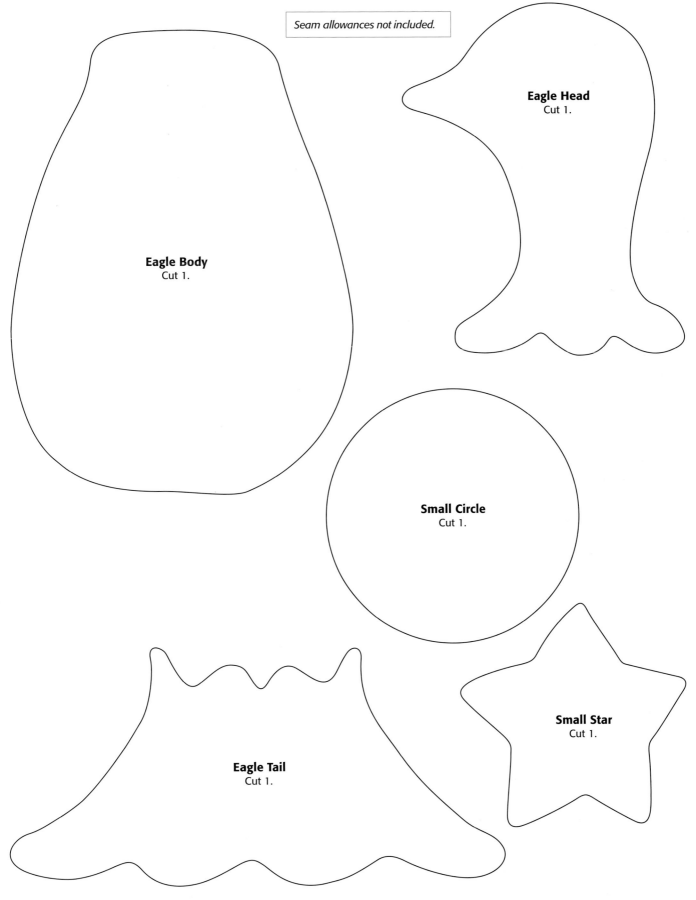

Seam allowances not included.

Eagle Head
Cut 1.

Eagle Body
Cut 1.

Small Circle
Cut 1.

Small Star
Cut 1.

Eagle Tail
Cut 1.

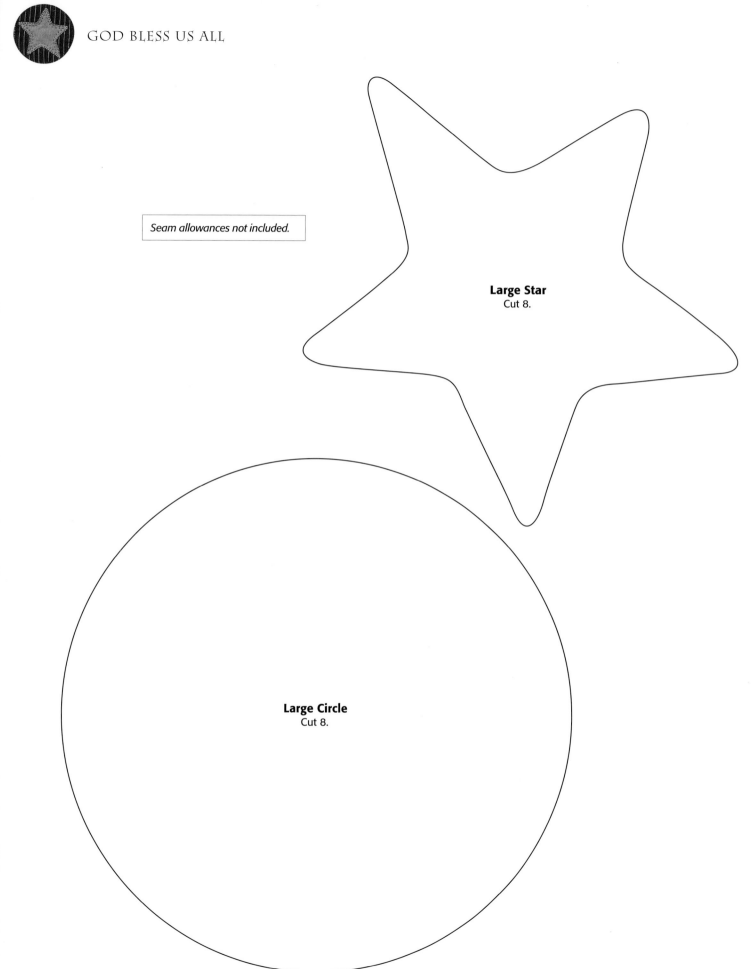

Seam allowances not included.

Large Star
Cut 8.

Large Circle
Cut 8.

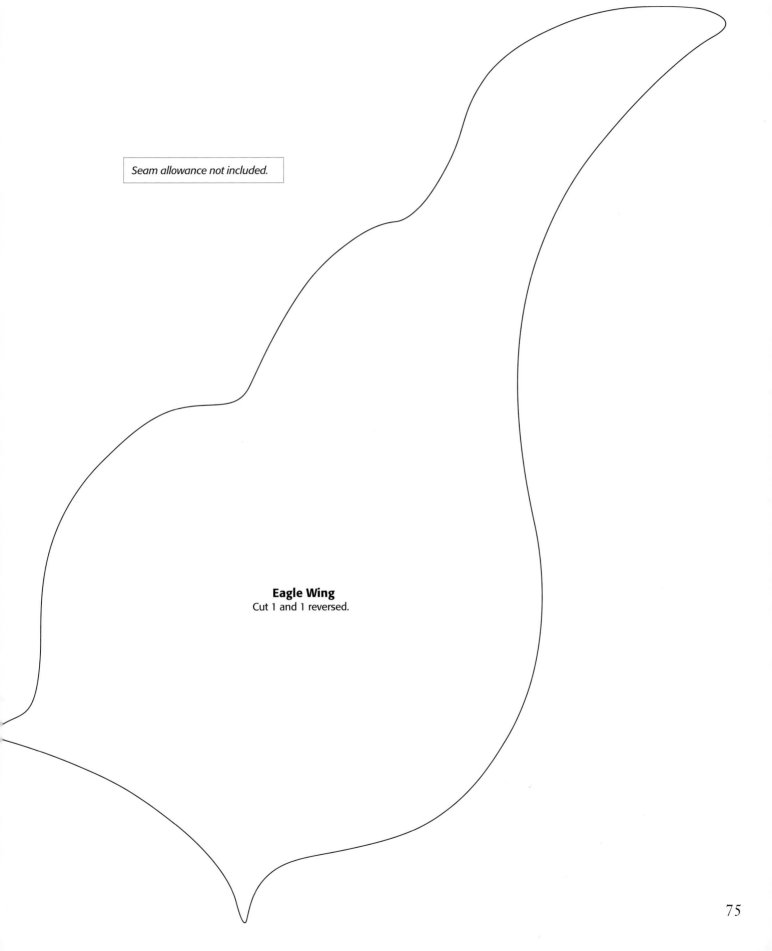

Seam allowance not included.

Eagle Wing
Cut 1 and 1 reversed.

Seam allowances not included.

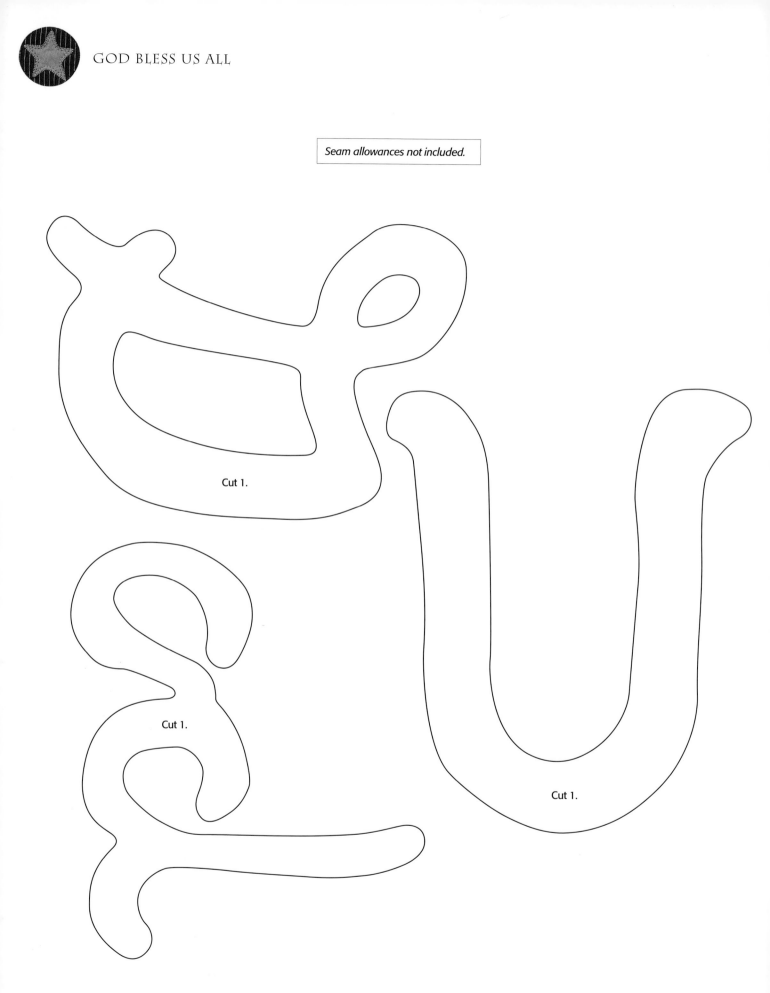

Cut 1.

Cut 1.

Cut 1.

Seam allowances not included.

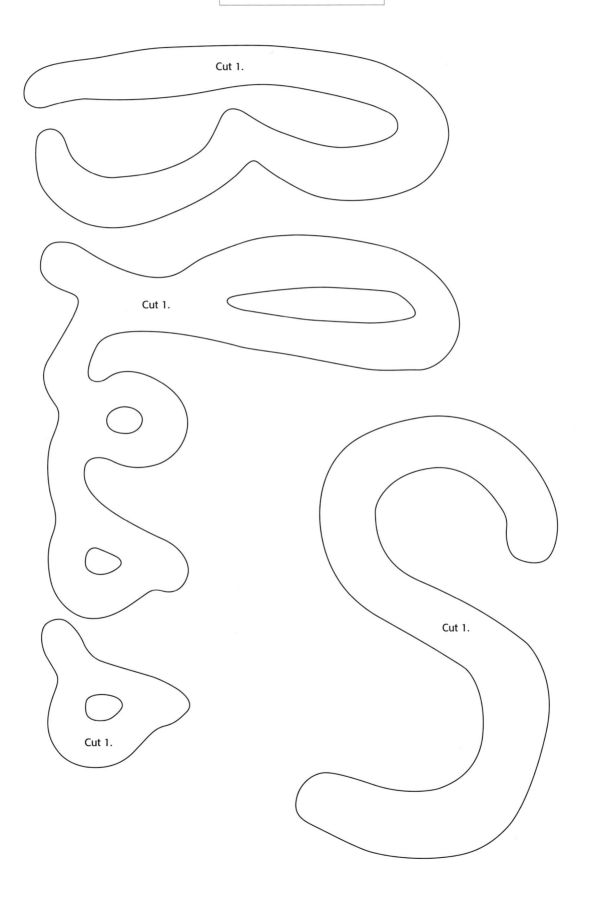

Cut 1.

Cut 1.

Cut 1.

Cut 1.

Seam allowances not included.

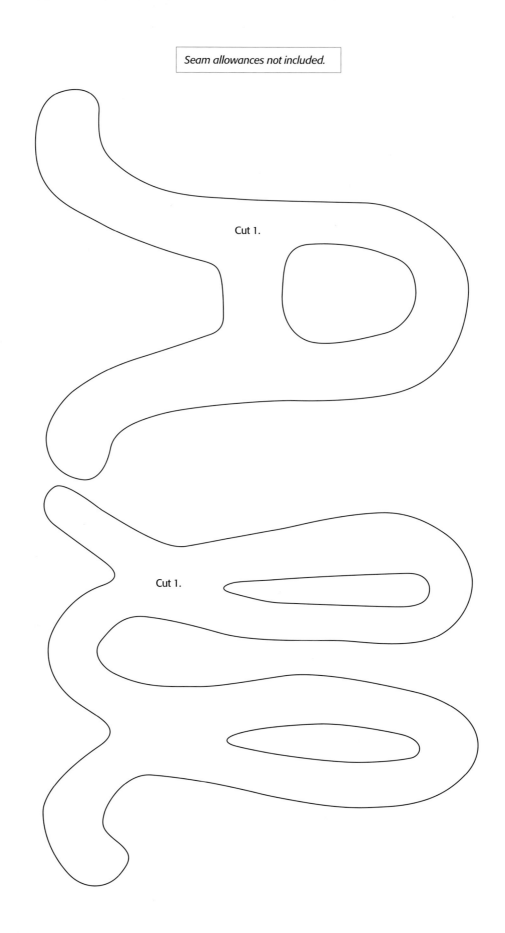

Cut 1.

Cut 1.

ABOUT THE AUTHOR

Tonee White lives in Scottsdale, Arizona, with her husband, Bob, and two of her seven children.

Tonee has been quilting for eleven years. She has written four books for That Patchwork Place, all of them featuring the appliquilt technique, which she developed.

Tonee teaches and lectures nationally, and from time to time her designs can be found in quilting magazines. She also enjoys rug hooking and is presently working on coordinating quilts and rugs for the home.

new and bestselling titles from

Martingale™
& COMPANY

America's Best-Loved Craft & Hobby Books™

 **That Patchwork Place®**

America's Best-Loved Quilt Books®

NEW RELEASES
Bear's Paw Plus
All through the Woods
American Quilt Classics
Amish Wall Quilts
Animal Kingdom CD-ROM
Batik Beauties
The Casual Quilter
Fantasy Floral Quilts
Fast Fusible Quilts
Friendship Blocks
From the Heart
Log Cabin Fever
Machine-Stitched Cathedral Stars
Magical Hexagons
Potting Shed Patchwork
Quilts from Larkspur Farm
Repliqué Quilts
Successful Scrap Quilts
   from Simple Rectangles

APPLIQUÉ
Artful Album Quilts
Artful Appliqué
Colonial Appliqué
Red and Green: An Appliqué Tradition
Rose Sampler Supreme

BABY QUILTS
Easy Paper-Pieced Baby Quilts
Even More Quilts for Baby: Easy as ABC
More Quilts for Baby: Easy as ABC
Play Quilts
The Quilted Nursery
Quilts for Baby: Easy as ABC

HOLIDAY QUILTS
Christmas at That Patchwork Place
Holiday Collage Quilts
Paper Piece a Merry Christmas
A Snowman's Family Album Quilt
Welcome to the North Pole

LEARNING TO QUILT
Basic Quiltmaking Techniques for:
   Borders and Bindings
   Divided Circles
   Hand Appliqué
   Machine Appliqué
   Strip Piecing
The Joy of Quilting
The Simple Joys of Quilting
Your First Quilt Book (or it should be!)

PAPER PIECING
50 Fabulous Paper-Pieced Stars
For the Birds
Paper Piece a Flower Garden
Paper-Pieced Bed Quilts
Paper-Pieced Curves
A Quilter's Ark
Show Me How to Paper Piece

ROTARY CUTTING
101 Fabulous Rotary-Cut Quilts
365 Quilt Blocks a Year Perpetual Calendar
Around the Block Again
Biblical Blocks
Creating Quilts with Simple Shapes
Flannel Quilts
More Fat Quarter Quilts
More Quick Watercolor Quilts
Razzle Dazzle Quilts

SCRAP QUILTS
Nickel Quilts
Scrap Frenzy
Scrappy Duos
Spectacular Scraps

CRAFTS
The Art of Stenciling
Baby Dolls and Their Clothes
Creating with Paint
The Decorated Kitchen
The Decorated Porch
A Handcrafted Christmas
Painted Chairs
Sassy Cats

KNITTING & CROCHET
Too Cute!
Clever Knits
Crochet for Babies and Toddlers
Crocheted Sweaters
Fair Isle Sweaters Simplified
Irresistible Knits
Knit It Your Way
Knitted Shawls, Stoles, and Scarves
Knitted Sweaters for Every Season
Knitting with Novelty Yarns
Paintbox Knits
Simply Beautiful Sweaters
Simply Beautiful Sweaters for Men
The Ultimate Knitter's Guide

Our books are available at bookstores and your favorite craft, fabric and yarn retailers. If you don't see the title you're looking for, visit us at www.martingale-pub.com or contact us at:

1-800-426-3126

International: 1-425-483-3313

Fax: 1-425-486-7596

E-mail: info@martingale-pub.com

For more information and a full list of our titles, visit our
Web site or call for a free catalog.